OUT
OF THE
DESERT

LUIS PALAU

two:twentypress

All Scripture quotations, unless otherwise indicated, are taken from the Holy Bible, New International Version®, NIV®, Copyright © 1973, 1978, 1984, 2011 by Biblica, Inc.™ Used by permission. All rights reserved worldwide.

Previous editions published as *So You Want to Grow, Steps Along the Way* (UK edition), and *Say Yes!*, copyright © 1984, 1986, 1995.

ISBN-10: 0985501901
ISBN-13: 978-0-9855019-0-7

Published by:
TWO:TWENTY PRESS
7914 East Maggie Court
Tucson, Arizona 85715

This title is also available in ebook format.
Visit www.LuisPalauBooks.com for more information.

Designer and cover photo: Curt Sell
Author photo: Tyler Gould

Printed in the United States of America

12 13 14 15 16 // TTP // 9 8 7 6 5 4 3 2 1

Endorsements

"God has used Luis in a tremendous way through many years. His friendship and support of me has meant more than he will ever know."

Billy Graham, Evangelist and Author

"It's obvious God has used Luis in a great way to fulfill His purposes for the Kingdom. I thank him for modeling that which matters most—transforming our world by changing lives through the abundant life found in Christ."

Rick Warren, New York Times bestselling author of *Purpose Driven Life*

"This book is as simple and invigorating as truth itself. That's because it is truth. It's the truth of the Gospel communicated in the winning, winsome, and wise voice of Luis Palau. Who doesn't desperately need to hear this? Who doesn't want the victorious life promised to us in Scripture? But how to get it? Here's how."

Eric Metaxas, New York Times bestselling author of *Bonhoeffer: Pastor, Martyr, Prophet, Spy*

"I remember the first time I saw Luis…what struck me was his genuine sense of concern for every person he came in touch with. It's something you can't fake. He's real."

President Bill Clinton

"I appreciate Luis Palau for bringing so many people together in fellowship and in celebration of faith, family, and values."

President George W. Bush

"My friend Luis Palau is one of the great evangelists of our age, with a gift for reaching people around the world."

Charles Colson, Founder of Prison Fellowship

"The strength of Palau's message…can be seen in the stadiums he fills."

TIME *magazine*

"One of the great joys of my life ministry has been to be a part of Luis Palau Festivals. I love so much the man…and the passion of the man… Luis Palau."

Steven Curtis Chapman, Grammy-award winning recording artist

"Luis's faithful commitment to the Gospel, and to the ongoing work of His Kingdom, has been exemplary. I praise God for the impact of his life."

Anne Graham Lotz, Evangelist and award-winning author of *Just Give Me Jesus*

"A listing of his campaigns reads like a world atlas: Jakarta, Kiev, Buenos Aires, San Antonio. He has preached on every continent except Antarctica. From Aberdeen, Scotland, to Zurich, Switzerland, Palau has tried to awaken cities to their need for God."

Associated Press

Contents

My soul clamors for God. It strains and groans. It cries out from the deep. It seeks communion with my Creator, my Savior—Yahweh. My soul beats for him…and it slumbers in wait. Awake, my soul. Awake. Arise to your Creator, your God. Rise up. Find strength to make your way out of your desert place. This is the beginning of your pilgrimage.

PREFACE

Without God, life has no meaning. Education has no purpose. Economics has no direction. Relationships have no foundation.

At least, that's what we're told. But is it true? Is life really all that different as a follower of Jesus Christ?

When we're honest with ourselves, do we really believe Jesus brings any lasting change to our lives? Or, as many are convinced, is faith in Jesus just some religious drug, resulting in a spiritual high for some time yet eventually leaving us confused, frustrated, and down-right despondent—stuck in the muck of habitual sin, working overtime to please God, and struggling to make sense of our dirty little lives?

After all, that's the life most of us know…and we know it well.

Things get tough. Obstacles come. And too often, the voice from above seems all too silent in the midst of our pain, our struggles, and our questions. You know the feeling….

Your prayers seem to hit the ceiling and bounce back at you with an ominous echo. Your situation at home or work goes from bad to worse, leaving you questioning your past decisions. Your relationships become strained, as if no one fully understands what you are going through. Your walk with God seems forced, distant, and anything but fruitful, causing you to wonder if you will ever know what this life is really all about.

How could you get it so wrong? How could you be so close, yet feel so far away? Why does this *normal* Christian life feel so unsettling, so bleak, so dry? How did you come to find yourself in this desert place and how in the world can you find your way out?

As you sit with Bible in hand, not knowing where to turn or what to read or how it relates to your life, you're left with serious, profound questions.

Where is God in the midst of your struggle?

Why doesn't he bring you lasting victory over sin?

Why are you fighting the same demons over and over again?

Why don't you have any joy?

Will you ever find relief this side of heaven, or are you forced to hang on bare-knuckled and pray it just doesn't get worse?

Like a majority of Jesus followers, I can only guess you have been through some serious trials in your life. And as you've struggled, you've wondered if what was sold to you as the *greatest gift in the world* really is more like *the greatest burden in the world.* It has become a set of rules. A constant feeling of condemnation. A continual reminder of your failures. And the last thing you feel is closeness with God.

You would never want to admit it, but in the back of your mind — in the quiet of night — you can't deny the feelings. Your joy is gone. Peace is foreign. And hope is fleeting away.

Does that sound at all familiar?

Deep down, you believe a successful, fruitful, God-centered life is possible. You wouldn't be on this journey if you didn't. You've even met others who seem to have it all together. Their lives give you hope. Their testimonies hint at something you desperately want. But your own searching and struggles have left you even more frustrated. And as you live in your never-ending cycle of backsliding behavior and unmet expectations — you are steps away from throwing your hands up in despair.

It's not that you're ready to turn your back on God. You know that's not the answer. You'll just continue on — frustrated and quiet, afraid to be honest or ask questions or share your ungodly feelings. You'll put on a smile, tell everyone life is good, and lower your hopes for something greater. You'll go to church. You'll give the right answers. You'll pray the right prayers, sing the right songs, and join the right small groups. Life will continue. But is that really what you want?

I challenge you to stop! Don't go there! Life doesn't have to be that way!

What if I told you that your struggles are common and your questions are valid? What if I told you I know just how you feel—lost in the shuffle and struggling to fully connect with God? What if I told you that I know the root of your personal unmet expectations and I have real, lasting solutions?

What if I told you that you didn't have to continue in frustration and shame and guilt and pain? What if I told you there are vital, simple steps you missed somewhere along the way that could set you free today—give you hope, and peace and joy— for eternity?

Would that change anything?

Please...hold on! Don't give up! You were made for more than this. There is a way out of this desert life. I know it's tough at times. Down-right frustrating at others. But you are not alone. Many have struggled through these same issues. And many have found success.

My simple thesis is this: you can find the way out of your own desert life. You can find the answer—the missing key—to your struggles and discouragement and pain. You can find direction. And most of all, you can discover hope for the life that God fully intended for you to live. And it all comes in a few simple, profound truths from scripture.

Your life can turn around. Your struggles can be overcome. Your questions, no matter how large or small, can find answers. Your frustrating, bare-boned, tear-you-up-inside experiences can be redeemed...now and for eternity. I promise you. I've been there. I know the questions. I understand the confusion. I understand there are days when it seems easier to just throw it all out the window and start something new.

This is that day. Not to throw it all away, but to start new. This is your day to set off down a new path and take a real, honest, authentic journey with God. This is your opportunity to lay it all out on the table, to hold nothing back—good or bad—and to see what the Lord really can do in your life when you are fully surrendered to him. (And when I say surrender, I don't mean what you think I mean.)

In the pages that follow, I am going to lay out some revolutionary truths that could radically change your life. Not just for today or for this week, but for eternity.

You can do this. And through my experiences—my raw, heart-wrenching, gut-check experiences over the past 60 years of life—I can help you.

Jesus is alive and active. He is ready and waiting to revolutionize your life. He was able to conquer the grave and he is able to redeem your story. He wants nothing more than to radically transform every area of your life. And if you let him, he will. Now hold on as I take you on the journey—from death to life; frustration to joy; apathy and pain to excitement and peace.

This is the beginning of your radical spiritual renewal out of the desert.

The Normal Christian Life

For several years after I met Jesus, I struggled. Sure, I started out well. The mountaintop experience. The endless pursuit of God. The hours of scripture reading and memorization and prayer. The bold proclamation of his truth—unashamedly sharing with my friends, family, and neighbors. I was ready to conquer the world, and I was only 12 years old.

Sadly, it didn't last long. My old self returned, and with a vengeance. I was moody, worried, fearful, and anxious.

No matter how hard I tried, I was lost in a valley. I saw little or no fruit in my life, and it lasted for years. The so-called "normal Christian life" I had heard so much about was replaced with frustration, shame, guilt, and fear, sprinkled with just enough brief interludes of joy to keep me wanting more.

Then, God woke me up.

He brought people into my life who helped walk me through

powerful, biblical steps toward a radical renewal of faith. The result—the Lord changed me into a joyful and fruitful servant of his. He picked me up from the ash heap of life and set me on a life of fulfillment and success. He showed me what a normal Christian life really should be—struggles and all. He met me in the desert and led me to freedom in him.

No doubt I'm still a work in progress. My goal, as Jesus so clearly stated, is to "be perfect, therefore, as your heavenly Father is perfect" (Matthew 5:48). Yet, I know I grieve the Holy Spirit and fail to display his fruit at times. And the fact is, I know my perfection will only be achieved the day I see my Savior face to face.

Even so, the difference in my life—as I have learned to trust God and draw near to him—has been dramatic, and I love him for the work he has done. Never have I felt this close to God. He is my guide, my provider, my all. He leads me daily. He sustains me constantly. And I know he'll do the same for you. He's just waiting…patiently…for you to be ready.

So, are you ready?

God wants nothing more than to bless your life beyond words—no matter your circumstances. That's why he sent his son. It's why he gave you the scriptures. Why he pursues you daily. He doesn't want you to struggle.

But this is a two-way street. He has called you to certain,

essential steps along the way. And frankly, you are driving blind. No wonder you have found yourself lost.

God has blessed my life beyond words. At times it has been in spite of myself. At others, it has been because of my obedience. But before I experienced any of that blessing, certain necessary and achievable steps were absolutely essential for my spiritual walk. They are steps that many of us skip over. We don't even think about them. We don't even realize they exist. That was never God's plan. After all, this is a journey—a sanctifying, God-honoring, eternally-minded process. A pilgrimage of the heart (Psalm 84:5). And he has things to teach us along the way.

These following pages clearly spell out many of those essential steps in which God is calling you. Just as God placed individuals in my life to teach me these valuable lessons, I pass them on to you. It is my hope that you may avoid the years of frustration I experienced and find true lasting victory in Jesus. The steps are simple, yet revolutionary for your life.

This book is packed with divinely revealed truth from God's Word. Not my words. His words. Words I have studied for more than 60 years. Words I have come to love and trust and understand on a deep, spiritual, jaw-dropping level. Anything I say is backed by scripture. If it's not, I give you full permission to use this book as kindling.

You can become a vibrant, victorious, cheerful, and dynamic

follower of Jesus. You can honor and exalt him in thought, word, and deed. It's not only possible, it's probable! I've seen it in the lives of many of my friends around the world.

And he wants nothing less for you.

IS EVERYBODY HAPPY...EXCEPT ME? 1

A surprising number of dissatisfied Christians fill our churches today. They don't necessarily look unhappy on the outside. In fact, they're often busy people, serving wherever they are needed. But when you explore behind the new clothes and plastic smiles, you discover that many people really don't enjoy being Christians.

And why should they?

For many, life has just become routine. There's no joy. No excitement. No victory. No peace. Quite frankly, their life doesn't seem all that much different from the atheist or agnostic down the street.

So the question for you is this…

Do *you* like being a Christian?

Or better said, are you satisfied with your life following Jesus?

It's a hard question, I know. Of course you believe Jesus is the way to victory. You don't question his existence or importance or relevance to your life. But, as you seek to follow him on a daily basis, are you feeling more frustrated than fulfilled?

Don't worry. I know the feeling. I felt exactly the same way for many years.

Losing My First Love

No one has adequately explained why anyone loses his or her initial joy and passion for the things of the Lord. But when I lost my first love of Jesus, it was as if someone pulled my plug and the lights went out.

Perhaps I let a cynical attitude get in the way. Maybe I ignored my mother's counsel to stay away from worldly influences. Or, perhaps I succumbed to the pressures of my fellow students. All I know is that one day, coming home from Bible club, I carelessly left my Bible on a streetcar and was unable to get it back. With that loss went my daily Bible reading, my attendance at Bible club, my excitement over Bible class, and almost everything that went along with my commitment to Jesus.

I still loved and believed and respected the gospel. I still remembered that day at age 12 in the mountains of Argentina when I gave my life over to God. Yet, like many, I became pretty good at not letting that one decision interfere with my daily life.

That negative, destructive attitude lasted four long years.

Since then, I've tried to determine just what went wrong. Essentially, I had no idea about how to live a victorious life. I had been taught the basics well, but I was into a spirituality based on performance. Praying, reading, studying, and going to church can wear thin quickly if that's all there is to a person's faith. I don't recall picking up any instruction on how to enjoy Jesus, how to walk with him, or how to be fully satisfied in him. I found myself bored with an endless repetition of the routine and an empty faith that left much to be desired.

And with one small speed bump, my walk with God was rocked to its core.

Though I take full responsibility, I know there were contributing factors to my detour in life. They are clear as day.

The first was that my father had not left a will when he died unexpectedly at age 35. I was just ten years old at the time, much too young to have any say about the family business. Several of my relatives stepped in, took over the business, and within three years ruined it, leaving us destitute. I was not equipped to forgive them, and the rage I felt as a young man was intense.

The rage became unbearable.

Second, there was the lure of the world and non-Christian friends. I was attracted to a life of parties and soccer games and listening to the radio—hardly bad things in themselves, but indicative of my loss of interest in the things of God.

My mother did everything she could to see that I continued in private school, but I was forced to live with my grandparents and commute to save money. It was humiliating. It also put me in a position to be less disciplined during my free time. Fortunately, even the non-Christian friends from my new neighborhood were pretty good kids, or I could have gotten into really big trouble.

Even though the family was nearly bankrupt and the business had virtually folded, I told my friends it was thriving and just waiting for me to come back to run it. I bragged about how I was going to be rich and powerful.

There was just one problem. I was lying.

By the time I was 16, I secretly blamed God for our troubles. I had come full circle—from love to blame. It tore me up inside.

The last straw was when my mother told me I could no longer continue in boarding school. I had dreamed of qualifying for the graduate program at Cambridge University, but I fell one year short. Instead, I finished with the equivalent of a junior college degree.

I felt like the victim of a cruel joke. Eight long, intensive years of training had left me with an intermediate degree, no money, and, as far as I could tell, no future.

I still feared God, but I questioned him daily. I was actually glad I had not served him more. I believed he owed me more than what I was getting, so why should I live for him? Deep down, I knew I was wrong. I knew I needed to return to him.

I never made fun of church, as some of my friends and relatives did. But I went sparingly, and then only to please my grandmother. I went late and left early, doing my best to appear uninterested. It wasn't difficult.

I joined the local university club and bought myself a pipe. (That's what the scholars did.) I studied a Dale Carnegie book and learned "how to win friends and influence people." I became a fast-talking, smooth-working phony.

Inside, I hated myself.

The turning point came just before Carnival Week in February. It was the week before Lent and would be followed by 40 days of confession and penance. Anything went. Any business not crucial to the festivities closed for the whole week. People partied. Rules were non-existent. Everyone, it seemed, got a free pass at life. Total abandon. I knew it would be my downfall.

I had grown tired of the sophisticated little parties and games the university club offered. Doing something more bizarre with my other friends sounded like an exciting alternative. So my friends and I made big plans for Carnival Week. Big, crazy, scary, clearly not God-honoring plans.

The more I thought about it, the more ominous it became. Somehow I knew if I went to Carnival Week, temptation would overwhelm me and I would be engulfed in sin.

I knew my mother and other relatives prayed daily that I would walk with the Lord. The more I thought about it the more panicky I became. If I participated in the carnival, I thought I could sever my relationship with the Lord completely. While in my head I knew nothing could separate me from the love of Jesus, in my heart I feared God might not forgive this out-and-out mockery of everything I had been taught.

I'm sure the Holy Spirit was convicting me. Toying with the world was one thing, but abandoning self-respect and flouting God's law was something else.

There was no purpose in my life, nothing to look forward to except more of the same empty "fun." If I went to Carnival Week, I was convinced I would go beyond the point of no return.

I had to get out of it.

My grandparents were gone that weekend and the house was empty. The next day my friends would come by to pick me up for the festivities. I was beside myself. I didn't have the strength to tell them I wasn't going. I had to have a reason. Falling to my knees by my bed, I pleaded with God: "Get me out of this and I will give up everything that's of the world. I will serve you and give my whole life to you. Just get me out of this!" I had no idea how God would get me out of my dilemma without my having to lie.

The next morning I awoke, slowly sat up, and swung my legs

over the side of the bed. I yawned, but my mouth felt strange. I touched it. I felt no pain, but could tell it was horribly swollen.

I stumbled to the mirror. My mouth was twice its normal size. Staring at my reflection, I worked up a crooked smile. No explanation. No clue what caused it. Yet it was clear in my mind— God had answered my prayer.

I called up one of my friends. "I can't go to the dance tonight, and I won't be going to the carnival at all this week," I said.

"Come on Luis. Everything has been planned."

"No. I have a good reason, and I will not go."

"You must be crazy! I'll be right over."

A few minutes later he showed up with three or four of the others. They insisted that the swelling would go down and that I should change my mind. But by then I had a good head of steam going and I resisted until they left.

I should have told my friends, that because of my faith in the Lord Jesus, I was afraid of the sin in which I might get involved. That's what I would tell them today. But I was so spiritually bankrupt it took that fat lip to deliver me from myself.

I thank God for that fat lip.

Knowing how good the gospel is, I am ashamed I was so cowardly. But at least I had made my decision, taken my stand, and broken with the world. I went back into the house, broke my pipe in two, tore up my university-club membership card, and threw away all my soccer and car-racing magazines and many record albums. None of those things were necessarily bad or evil in-and-of themselves. But they had clearly become idols to me. They were standing in the way of a truly fruitful life with Jesus and I had had enough.

I was a new man.

The next day I went to church morning and night. The rest of the town, it seemed, was frolicking in sin. I was glad to have escaped. Everything seemed different. I was excited. Life perked up and had meaning once again.

Looking back, I'm so thankful for the promise of Philippians 1:6, "I am sure that God who began the good work within you will keep right on helping you grow in his grace until his task within you is finally finished on that day when Jesus Christ returns" (TLB).

Slowly I was seeing, that although I might fail God many times in my life, he would never fail me. I was learning, step-by-step, what it meant to live a godly, joyful, fruitful life. And he was just getting started.

The most crucial step, however, was still ahead. Almost eight years later, God would smack me upside the head once again. And this time, my life would truly take off.

Trying Too Hard

After dedicating my life to Jesus, some of my teenage friends and I started all-night prayer meetings each Friday. We wanted to prove we really meant business. We'd take coffee and cookies to stay awake during the early morning hours. We confessed our sins, laid hands on each other, read promises, prayed for the lost, prayed for the church. Mostly, we prayed about temptations we didn't know how to handle.

Whenever a great preacher came to our church, our small group would try to get an interview with him. Our questions were always the same:

- How can we get victory over temptation?

- How can we live holy lives?

- What do we have to do?

Usually the visiting preacher would ask, "Are you reading the Bible?"

"Yes, we get up at 5:00 every morning before going to school or work. We read several chapters every day."

"Great. But are you testifying for Jesus?"

"Yes. We hand out tracts, teach children's classes, and even hold street meetings."

"That's terrific. But are you praying?" the preacher would ask. So we'd tell him all about our all-night prayer meetings.

Our frustration must have been obvious. "What else do we need to do?" we'd ask.

"Well, pray some more, witness some more, and read the Bible some more."

So we did. We just about killed ourselves we were so eager to be holy. And the results never changed.

Others would urge us from the pulpit to rededicate our lives to Jesus Christ. So we went forward. But I would still have many of the same feelings of frustration and inadequacy. *Maybe there's some area of my life I still haven't dedicated to the Lord,* I thought. So I would go to the alter once again. Standing before the pulpit, I would re-rededicate my life. Then, a year later, I would re-rededicate my life. But it still wasn't working.

Some of my friends started dropping out of our all-night prayer meetings. Others stopped going to church altogether. Some slipped out quietly, others ended up in blatant sin. But we all had a sense of despair.

"We've read the Bible like mad. We've prayed all night. We've shared the gospel whenever possible, but we still can't say no to certain temptations."

"Either the gospel doesn't work," one of my friends concluded, "or I'm such a sinner that even God can't help me."

Another friend cynically made fun of the verses that speak of Christian victory. When I ran across a good book on the subject, my friend said, "I'd like to see how victorious that author would be if he were under a broken-down car with oil dripping on his face." I couldn't argue with him. I felt the same way. And cynicism crept in.

I hung in there...barely. I loved the scriptures and studied them diligently. But I never got the point of knowing what it meant to walk in the Spirit without being legalistic. I longed to be free of the self-effort of the flesh. My times of study and prayer and work became a cycle of grim determination. I knew the power came from the Spirit, but for some reason I didn't experience it. I continued to search desperately, when I should have long since found it.

I was on the verge of giving up. Not because I saw any lack in God, but because I was weary of fighting and struggling and seeking to persevere through sheer dedication. I was exhausted, and exhaustion can breed cynicism.

When am I ever going to catch on? I wondered. Will I give up now after all I've been through? I knew the other side of life was hopeless. But there is a monumental emptiness when you know you're looking in the right place and still not finding the answer. I wanted to please and love and serve God. I wanted people to be saved. I would sing, "Oh, Jesus, I have promised to serve Thee to the end," and I would think, *even if it kills me.*

One day I was invited to hear someone speak about the possibility of a Billy Graham campaign in Argentina. What impressed me most—besides the size of the crowd—was a brief film of Dr. Graham speaking to Christian leaders in India.

The film showed an unbelievable crowd of tens of thousands of people. There on the screen—Dr. Graham poured out his soul. As he stared into the camera, I felt he was staring directly at me.

He was preaching from Ephesians 5:18—"Do not get drunk on wine, which leads to debauchery. Instead, be filled with the Spirit."

It was as if the crowd in India didn't exist. He was looking right at me and shouting, "Are you filled with the Spirit? Are *you* filled with the Spirit? Are you filled with the Spirit?"

I knew that was my problem. I wasn't filled with the Spirit. That was the reason for my up-and-down Christianity. That's why I had zeal and commitment, but little fruit or victory.

When would it end? When would I find the answer? I found it in the United States after several frustrating months of graduate-level theological studies.

No Longer I

I came to the States through the patient prodding of the late Ray Stedman, then pastor of Peninsula Bible Church in Palo Alto, California. The first two months, I lived in his home. I was argumentative and wanted to discuss theology and doctrine for hours. I had come to learn, but I clearly wasn't yet ready to admit, that I didn't have all the answers. Ray and Elaine and their four daughters were so patient and understanding. Their harmony pervaded the place, despite the fiery Latino who had invaded their home. Ray's humor kept everyone happy and we all became fast friends.

Two months with the Stedmans wasn't enough time to learn American culture—how to chat and eat and behave the way the natives do—but it was all I had before going north to Multnomah Biblical Seminary (now Multnomah University) in Portland, Oregon. Multnomah is a demanding school, and I found the first semester particularly rough.

What made it most frustrating was Dr. George Kehoe, our Spiritual Life class professor. He began every class by quoting Galatians 2:20—"I have been crucified with Christ and I no longer live, but Christ lives in me. The life I live in the body, I live by faith in the Son of God, who loved me and gave himself for me."

I was still struggling in my own little argument with God. I was frustrated that no matter how hard I tried I was not able to live out the lifestyle I saw in men like Ray Stedman and several others at Peninsula Bible Church. Their lives were filled with real joy and freedom. But the more I sought it, the more elusive it became.

My spiritual journey seemed like a climb up a tall cliff. I clawed every inch of the way uphill only to slip back down. Although I had experienced times of blessing and victory, for the most part the struggle seemed impossible. I couldn't go on that way, especially when no one else knew about it.

It was my secret, private death.

I wondered how long I could hold on to the side of the cliff. Eventually, my will would give out. My strength would be gone. If I didn't get help soon, I was going to let go altogether.

I felt like a sincere hypocrite. People laugh when I say that, but I truly was, and it wasn't funny.

Some hypocrites know they are hypocrites and want to be that way. They want to have two lives—one to show off at church and one to live in private. I simply wanted to be the person people thought I was.

If I were to describe myself in those days, I would have to say I was envious, jealous, preoccupied, self-centered, and ambitious to a wrong degree. I was smug about other speakers, silently rating their illustrations or delivery against my own. That left me feeling mean and ugly and petty. No amount of wrestling with myself would rid me of those sins. And yet I tried. I felt despicable. I hated the idea of being a hypocrite.

Maybe that's why I didn't like the constant reminder of Galatians 2:20. I was getting so annoyed at Dr. Kehoe's quoting that verse every day that I had to ask myself why. *It can't be a Bible verse that gets you so upset*, I told myself. It must be you. Yet rather than let that verse penetrate my pride, I decided instead that the verse was self-contradictory, hard to understand, and confusing, especially in English.

Any Old Bush

Shortly before Christmas break, a visitor spoke at one of our chapel services. I had taken to sitting in the back of the auditorium during daily chapel, where we usually got another dose of exposition or missionary stories. I dared the speaker to make me pay attention. If he was good, I'd honor him by listening. Otherwise, I would daydream or peek at my class notes.

That day, the speaker was Major Ian Thomas. He was founder and general director of the Torchbearers, the group that runs the Capernwray Hall Bible School in England. His British accent and staccato delivery were unusual, but what really intrigued me was the way he pointed at us with a finger that had been partially amputated. While his speaking style hooked me, his short message shook me to the core.

I was locked in.

Major Ian Thomas talked about Moses and how it took this great man 40 years in the wilderness to learn that he was nothing. Then one day, Moses was confronted with a burning bush. Thomas said that the burning bush in the desert was likely a dry bunch of ugly little sticks that had hardly developed, yet Moses had to take off his shoes.

Why? Because this was holy ground.

Why? Because God was in the bush!

Here was Major Thomas' point. God was telling Moses, "I don't need a pretty bush or an educated bush or an eloquent bush. Any old bush will do, as long as I am in the bush. If I am going to use you, I am going to use you. It will not be you doing something for me, but me doing something through you."

It suddenly hit me like a ton of bricks. I was that kind of bush: a worthless, useless bunch of dried-up sticks. I could do nothing for God. All my reading and studying and asking questions and trying to model myself after others was worthless. Everything in my ministry was worthless, unless God was in the bush. Only he could make something happen. Only he could make it work.

Thomas told of many Christian workers who failed at first because they thought they had something to offer God. He himself had once imagined that because he was an aggressive, winsome, evangelistic sort, God would use him. But God didn't use him until he came to the end of himself. *That's exactly my situation,* I thought.

I was—no doubt—at the end of myself.

Thomas closed his message by reading Galatians 2:20. It all came together for me.

"I have been crucified with Christ and I no longer live, but Christ lives in me."

That was it. Like a weight lifted off my shoulders, it all came together. I no longer live. Jesus is in me. I would finally let God be God and let Luis Palau depend on him. It was as simple as that.

You can't imagine the complete release I felt. I ran back to my room and in tears fell to my knees next to my bunk. "Lord, now I understand!" I prayed. "The whole thing is 'not I, but Christ in me.' It's not what I'm going to do for you, but rather what you're going to do through me."

I stayed on my knees until lunchtime, talking with God. I realized the reason I hated myself inside was because I wrongly loved myself outside. I asked God's forgiveness for my pride. I had thought I was really something, but God was not active in my life. I hadn't given him the chance.

Well, God still had a lot of burning to do, but he was finally in control. He wanted me to be grateful for all the small things he had put in my life, but he didn't want me to place my confidence in those opportunities. He wanted me to depend not on myself or my breaks, but on Jesus alone—the indwelling, resurrected, almighty Lord Jesus.

I was thrilled to finally realize I have everything I need when I have Jesus literally living in me. My inner resource is God himself because of my union with Jesus (see Colossians 2:9-15). It's his power that controls my disposition, enables me to serve, and corrects and directs me (see Philippians 2:13). Out of this understanding comes a godly sense of self-worth. And it's your reality as well.

That day marked the intellectual turning point in my spiritual life.

The practical working out of that discovery would be lengthy and painful, but at last the realization had come. It was exciting beyond words. I could relax and rest in Jesus. He was going to do the work through me. What peace there was in knowing I could quit struggling!

I soon discovered, however, that my struggles weren't unique. One way or another, many Christians live the way I lived all those years. They've given their hearts to Jesus. They've received him. They love him. But they can't seem to make the Christian life work the way they thought it was supposed to work.

Sure, they hang in there. They show up at church. They're part of the 20 percent who do 80 percent of the work in most local churches. Or they're part of the 60 percent who used to be active but for now just fill the pews. They have little joy, little freedom, little fruit. In a moment of honesty, they'll admit they're not happy.

Maybe you're there.

I meet unhappy, discouraged, and defeated Christians almost anywhere I go. I have to ask—Is this really what Jesus had in mind when he came and died on the cross for our sins? Is this really what he was thinking when he rose again—overcoming death? Was this really his hope for us when he said, "You shall receive power when the Spirit comes on you, and you shall be my witnesses" (Acts 1:8) or when he asserted that "out of your inmost being shall flow rivers of living water" (John 7:38)?

Or are some folks missing the whole point?

As I look back on my life and my own spiritual journey, I've come to understand there were several foundational spiritual truths I had completely overlooked. Finally understanding these truths led to my own spiritual renewal.

Now I want to share them with you.

TREMENDOUS POSSIBILITIES 2

It started as the internationally acclaimed maiden voyage of the world's largest, most luxurious ship. It ended as the greatest of sea tragedies. It's said that one-way passage in one of the ship's finest suites cost the equivalent of $50,000 in today's funds. At the length of nearly 883 feet and 66,000 tons displacement, the S.S. Titanic truly lived up to its name.

Today, the S.S. Titanic is not known for its success or grandeur or luxurious living. Instead, most people today who hear the word "titanic" immediately think of a rusting hulk of a ship lying at the bottom of the Atlantic Ocean some six hundred miles off the coast of Nova Scotia. It's known for the tragic disaster that took the lives of hundreds of innocent people.

Ironically, it is said that efforts by the S.S. Titanic's crew to avert hitting the now famous iceberg proved disastrous. According to many, had the ship stayed on course, only two or three compartments would have flooded and it would have remained afloat. Instead, more than 1,500 people lost their lives.

So much promise.

Such needless tragedy.

I'm reminded of the S.S. Titanic when I think of the lives of countless hundreds of thousands of people who claim to be Christians but aren't enjoying the Christian life. They talk about going to heaven but they look like…well…someplace else.

Isn't the new life we received in Jesus far better than the old life we left behind? Think about it.

If you're a real Christian, isn't your future secure? Aren't your sins forgiven? Aren't you indwelt by God?

If all that's true, why are we not enjoying victory over sin? Are we holy people? Do others sense the presence of God in our lives? If not, no wonder we lack the courage to share God's Good News with those still far from God. No wonder we sometimes feel the gospel is only a call to frustration and disillusionment.

Before we trusted the Lord Jesus Christ as Savior, we were without hope and without God. Like everybody else, we had no victory over the world, the flesh, or the devil. We knew nothing of the joy and power that comes from a holy life. God was nothing more than an idea or rumor. We were on a collision course for hell.

But when we put our faith and trust in Jesus, everything changed. We now know God. We love him. And we will spend all eternity with him.

Yet, are we viewing salvation in too small a way? The fact is…

• God indwells us…now.

• He came to give us life…now.

- He came to bring us peace…now.

- He came to redeem us from hell…now.

Our hope is for eternity…and for right now. Yet sadly, many of us forget that fact. We have been blessed with every spiritual blessing. Like the psalmist David, our head should be anointed with the oil of the Holy Spirit and our cup should be running over (Psalm 23:5). We should be the happiest and holiest of people, drawing others to the Lord.

But is that the case?

The Lord says he's given us his peace, but we still wrestle with worry and restlessness. God commands us to rejoice, but discouragement and depression overwhelm us at times. He tells us to love one another, but we often feel either critical or criticized. We're exhorted to glorify the Lord, but when push comes to shove we end up dishonoring him and feeling guilty instead.

Scripture says if God is for us, who can be against us? But hardship and tragedy still strike those called by his name. The Bible promises that God gives his children good gifts, but we sometimes feel left out. We read about "streams of living water" (John 7:38) flowing out of our innermost being, but the joy of the Holy Spirit seldom flows out of our lives.

Is your cup running over this week? Is my cup running over?

Or do we quietly ache for a radical touch of God in our lives?

Do you remember how you felt when you first became a Christian? I could hardly sleep that night. I was so excited about committing my life to Jesus. I knew it was the most important decision I would ever make.

The first days of my Christian life were like the spectacular bonfires we built each night at camp—flames shooting toward the sky. But gradually, the inner fire in my soul died down. Underneath the ashes of my façade were a few live coals, but from the outside, I appeared cold. After going through a deep spiritual crisis several years later, I finally began to experience God's renewal in my life. Gradually, kindling and fresh logs were added, the sparks were fanned, and the flame returned. But how I wished that renewal had begun much sooner!

This book is about renewal—how to get the fire of God blazing again in our lives. Renewal is the greatest need in the church today. What is renewal? It's God himself in action, working in and through us. When we're renewed, our love for him is rekindled. We love his people. The Word of God becomes alive to us again. We gain a vision for evangelism, a burden for the lost. And temptation loses its grip on our affections.

Such renewal touches every aspect of our lives. It doesn't depend on carefully orchestrated circumstances or special revival conferences to work us up to some "mountain top" experience.

Some people claim, "I could be happy if life treated me right." But the fact is: life isn't fair. We all go through rough, sometimes devastating circumstances. Yet the evidence is overwhelming that we can know the joy of the Lord all the same.

I think the problem many Christians have is that they don't believe the incredible possibilities available through experiencing God's radical renewal. It really is radical—by that I mean it's fundamental and extreme. God himself wants you to discover what it truly means to enjoy the Christian life, even in life's worst situations.

So what is the potential of radical renewal in Jesus? It is a life that is triumphant and victorious; transparent and holy; completely dominated by God himself.

Renewal Is Triumphant, Victorious Living

We all have different temperaments—different ways we approach life. Some of us are optimistic, others a bit more pessimistic. Some of us are outgoing, others more introverted. Some of us are easy-going, others tend to take life more seriously. Those differences are part of our natural makeup as human beings.

But Scripture teaches all Christians—whatever their temperament—can be victorious, Spirit-filled, joyful. That's supposed to be the normal Christian life. I love how the apostle Paul pictures it: "Thanks be to God, who in Christ always leads us in triumph, and through us spreads the fragrance of the knowledge of him everywhere" (2 Corinthians 2:14 RSV).

Notice what Paul says: "God...leads us in triumph." And the result? Others sense the fragrance of Jesus in our lives. That fragrance permeates the air around any Christian who has experienced radical renewal and who has a passion for the things of God.

The word triumph implies warfare, and we are indeed engaged in spiritual warfare. In this war, one side is going to win and the other side is going to lose. The fact Christians are led by God in victory doesn't mean we have it easy. It's war out there, and warfare is never pleasant.

Frankly, it's the war raging about us that makes the Christian life exciting, much as a hard-fought athletic event is exciting to the athletes who participate. In this war, we don't accommodate our foes or pacify them. We certainly don't give up when the battle gets fierce. And, in this war, we never accept defeat. We're horrified at that thought. We rebel against it. Instead, we gain victory over our enemies through our Lord Jesus Christ and his victory won on the cross.

Victory Over the World

Scripture speaks of three enemies we do battle with. The first of these enemies is the world. I happened to grow up in a church that forever blasted the world. They believed drab was beautiful and that sports and parties were a waste of time. They shunned anything that appeared worldly. I never thought God's Word might have another perspective.

What does the Bible mean by the world, anyway? As you read the Bible, especially the New Testament, it's amazing how it seems to personify this enemy. When Scripture mentions the world, of course, it isn't talking about this planet. It's describing everyone on earth who doesn't know God and, more broadly, their dominating philosophy and way of life.

Though we live in the midst of this present world system, God never intended that we expend all of our energy fighting this one enemy. That was a mistake I saw as I was growing up; we were constantly warned about the evils of certain music, certain people, and certain activities. Paradoxically, I found myself so caught up fighting the world at times that I ended up flustered by the flesh and defeated by the devil.

Of course, we shouldn't sit around and let the world squeeze us into its mold, either. Many Christians fall for the world because they forget we're at war with it. I don't mean we're at war with the people of this world. We're supposed to love them, as God does. But we should hate the whole ugly, arrogant, self-centered, ego-building, pride-engendering system that's out to destroy the lives of those around us.

The world comes at us constantly, even when we're not aware of it. I happen to have a remote control gadget for my television set and can bang through all the channels as I walk through our living room. Sometimes it seems like almost everything that's on, even news and sports, is a pain and a problem. The world is propagating its message from every angle imaginable, 24 hours a day. Are we critically interacting with it, or passively accepting anything that's thrown at us by the media?

In 1 John 2:15-17 we read: "Do not love the world or anything in the world. If anyone loves the world, the love of the Father is not in him. For everything in the world—the cravings of sinful man, the lust of his eyes and the boasting of what he has and does—comes not from the Father but from the world. The world and its desires pass away, but the man who does the will of God lives forever."

Fortunately our victory over the world is sure. Why? Because "greater is he who is in you than he who is in the world" (1 John 4:4 NASB). The Lord Jesus himself reminded his disciples: "In this world you will have trouble. But take heart! I have overcome the world" (John 16:33). So there's a war going on between the desires of the world and the will of God. We all feel it. But we can triumph in that conflict by the power of Jesus.

All the power of the risen, living Lord Jesus is available to you and me in this war with the world. That doesn't mean the world's appeal will melt away. We need to remember that until we meet the Lord someday, we're still living in enemy territory.

But "though we live in the world, we do not wage war as the world does. The weapons we fight with are not the weapons of the world. On the contrary, they have divine power to demolish strongholds" (2 Corinthians 10:3-4).

What are some of the strongholds of the world? Paul tells us: "We demolish arguments and every pretension that sets itself up against the knowledge of God, and we take captive every thought to make it obedient to Christ" (2 Corinthians 10:5). So a stronghold is anything that says no to God, that denies his rule and authority. Attitudes like apathy, materialism, pride, and the worship of self. Add to that philosophies like humanism, secularism, and rationalism. Then there are false religions or, as 1 Timothy 4:1 says, the teachings of demons, which are so prevalent today.

These strongholds of the world have an incredible grip on our society, as evidenced in the media, yet they're no match for God's power at work in us. But there's another more subtle enemy we also have to contend with.

Victory Over the Flesh

The second enemy we're at war with is the flesh. Now, flesh means more than just our bodies, though our physical frame often is the center of the battlefield. Some translate this term "sinful nature." Others speak of our "old nature." In any case, this much is clear: as Christians, we have a terrible enemy entrenched within us.

The flesh is at war within us, opposing the Holy Spirit who indwells us. As Christians, we are exhorted to "live by the Spirit and you will not gratify the desires of the sinful nature. For the sinful nature desires what is contrary to the Spirit, and the Spirit what is contrary to the sinful nature" (Galatians 5:16-17).

In the very next paragraph of Galatians it's clear the works of the flesh have no place in the life of the believer. The list is graphic: "sexual immorality, impurity and debauchery; idolatry and witchcraft; hatred, discord, jealousy, fits of rage, selfish ambition, dissensions, factions and envy; drunkenness, orgies, and the like." We are warned that "those who live like this will not inherit the kingdom of God" (Galatians 5:21).

Nevertheless, any of us in the church can be deceived by this enemy. We're easily impressed by good looks, show business, and emotional excesses. We're often fooled when the flesh passes itself off as being religious when actually it's acting in a debased or treacherous manner toward others.

In contrast, "the fruit of the Spirit is love, joy, peace, patience, kindness, goodness, faithfulness, gentleness and self-control. Against such things there is no law" (Galatians 5:22-23). Why isn't there a law against the fruit of the Spirit? Because we can never love too much, or have too much joy or peace.

There's a very real battle within us. If we give in to the lusts of the flesh, we automatically grieve the Holy Spirit and quench his work within us. But that doesn't have to be the case in our lives. We can know victory on this battlefront, too! Paul reminds us that "we have an obligation—but it is not to the sinful nature, to live according to it" (Romans 8:12).

We're all at war with this enemy. It destroys many Christians. But it doesn't have to. The question is, are you overcoming the flesh? By the power of the Holy Spirit your answer can be an emphatic yes!

Victory Over the Devil

There's a third enemy—the devil. The Bible also calls him Satan, Lucifer, the adversary, the deceiver. A lot of people, even in Christian circles, caricature him and think he's laughable. But, as we all find out sooner or later, the devil is a vicious enemy.

The Lord Jesus put it bluntly: "He [the devil] was a murderer from the beginning, not holding to the truth, for there is no truth in him. When he lies, he speaks his native language, for he is a liar and the father of lies" (John 8:44).

The difference between Satan and our Savior couldn't be greater. "The thief [again referring to the devil] comes only to steal and kill and destroy; I [Jesus] have come that they may have life, and have it to the full" (John 10:10).

Peter warns us, "Your enemy the devil prowls around like a

roaring lion looking for someone to devour. Resist him, standing firm in the faith, because you know that your brothers throughout the world are undergoing the same kind of sufferings" (1 Peter 5:8-9).

James adds, "Resist the devil, and he will flee from you. Come near to God and he will come near to you. Wash your hands, you sinners, and purify your hearts, you double-minded" (James 4:7-8).

Paul urges us to put on spiritual armor in order to protect ourselves from this enemy, "Finally, be strong in the Lord and in his mighty power. Put on the full armor of God so that you can take your stand against the devil's schemes. For our struggle is not against flesh and blood, but against the rulers, against the authorities, against the powers of this dark world and against the spiritual forces of evil in heavenly realms. Therefore put on the full armor of God, so that when the day of evil comes, you may be able to stand your ground, and after you have done everything, to stand" (Ephesians 6:10-13).

There's no demilitarized zone in the midst of this war. Either we're standing in the strength of God's power or we're knocked down in defeat. There's no room for pride, for thinking we can walk a line somewhere between the kingdom of darkness and the kingdom of light.

Are you living in victory against the devil? Can you say, "Thanks be to God, who in Christ always leads us in triumph"?

Or are you experiencing failure and defeat? Perfection is impossible until we get to heaven, but we can experience ongoing victory over the world, the flesh, and the devil. That's the first great possibility before us.

Renewal is Transparent, Holy Living

Scripture also teaches the Christian life is a transparent, holy life. The Bible says, "As obedient children, do not conform to the evil desires you had when you lived in ignorance. But just as he who called you is holy, so be holy in all you do; for it is written: 'Be holy, because I am holy'" (1 Peter 1:14-16).

The Bible also says, "Make every effort to live in peace with all men and to be holy; without holiness no one will see the Lord" (Hebrews 12:14). And John reminds us, "If we walk in the light, as he is in the light, we have fellowship with one another, and the blood of Jesus, his Son, purifies us from all sin" (1 John 1:7).

What does it mean to be holy and transparent? Holiness means to live in the light with God. It means to walk in accordance with all we've learned in the Word and all that the Holy Spirit teaches us. In other words, it's a commitment to purity.

Transparency means, as far as I know, I don't have anything to hide from my heavenly Father. Furthermore, there is nothing between me and anyone else that I haven't tried to settle from my side of things—even if the other person doesn't want to settle the issue.

Holiness isn't a movement or annual convention; it can be our vital, daily experience. Transparency doesn't mean absolute perfection, though that is the goal. We must never lower the standard the Lord Jesus gave his disciples: "Be perfect, therefore, as your heavenly Father is perfect" (Matthew 5:48). We must never make room for sin, even though we're fully aware we sometimes do fail the Lord.

Some of God's holiest and most honored servants actually found they became more aware of their imperfections as they drew closer to the Lord. They lamented their sinfulness, even though they weren't committing any terrible, wicked deeds of the flesh. As the Holy Spirit scrutinized their lives, they saw even their smallest faults as massive sins. And they longed for the day of Christ when God's good work within them would be complete (Philippians 1:6) and they would be holy like Jesus (1 John 3:2).

We see this in Paul's descriptions of himself. Toward the end of his life, he called himself the worst of sinners (1 Timothy 1:15). That wasn't hyperbole; that was based on objective fact. Paul had ransacked the church and committed the most violent of crimes before his conversion.

But Paul also rejoiced in God's complete forgiveness and actively pursued holiness. He could say, "Not that I have...

already been made perfect, but I press on to take hold of that for which Christ Jesus took hold of me" (Philippians 3:12). Lack of perfection didn't stop Paul from living as transparently as possible. Why? Because he was conscious of the fear of the Lord, and because he longed for the day when he would see his Lord face to face.

Are you holy? Am I holy? Are we enjoying the freedom of a transparent conscience? Can we honestly say, "Lord, I praise your name that there's nothing to hide from you. I'm not covering up anything. I'm walking in the light. My soul is clean. My conscience is transparent. So far as I know, there's nothing I need to settle with anyone. Lord, I love you and I thank you there isn't a cloud between you and me."

Such a statement is your privilege as a Christian. It's the great offer of the gospel. The point of Christianity, to a great measure, is that God loves us and wants us to enjoy the freedom of relating to him in holiness and transparency. His delight is that we walk in the light, that we live holy and happy lives in him. Is that our experience, or is there something that's getting in the way?

Today we're bombarded by the world and its way of thinking. We're continually enticed to cross the line, to give in to the flesh, to pledge alliance to the devil. Often, we're not even aware of what's happening.

The world is great at promoting its own agenda and ideas.

Men and women have made careers out of listening to people's problems and offering advice. Others write newspaper columns or appear on talk shows. And sometimes what they have to say sounds pretty good.

But good advice isn't good enough. God's Good News is the radical power of the Lord Jesus Christ. He doesn't offer us advice; he offers us power to live holy and transparently in a corrupt and deceitful age.

I know some people react and say, "Come on. I've heard all this talk before. Victorious Christian living? What a cliché! Walking in the light with a clear conscience? What a joke! You can try to make it sound good, but it doesn't work for me."

When a person says something like that, it reveals two things about his or her character. First, that person doesn't have a clear conscience. And second, he or she has become cynical. Cynicism is the language of the devil, and it leads to depression.

It shouldn't be surprising that many cynical saints are depressed. The fragrance of Jesus is missing in their lives. They've lost their first love for the Lord. They've lost the joy and peace Jesus brings. And in place of a passion for the lost, they've become critical or at least skeptical of the church and the things of God.

Thankfully, God has provided a mechanism for forgiveness for contaminated consciences. We'll consider that in more detail later. First, however, there's one more tremendous possibility of the Christian life to consider.

Renewal is a Total Lifestyle

The heart of the New Testament teaches that the Christian life is a total lifestyle dominated by God himself. To me, this is the most exciting possibility imaginable. No wonder Paul prayed earnestly that "out of his [the Father's] glorious riches he may strengthen you with power through his Spirit in your inner being, so that Christ may dwell in your hearts through faith" (Ephesians 3:16-17).

Listen to the rest of Paul's prayer: "I pray that you, being rooted and established in love, may have power, together with all the saints [and that includes you and me], to grasp how wide and long and high and deep is the love of Christ, and to know this love that surpasses knowledge—that you may be filled to the measure of all the fullness of God" (Ephesians 3:17-19).

Did you catch that last phrase? "That you may be filled to the measure of all the fullness of God." Imagine how different your life would be if you were completely, totally filled with God himself. No area of your life would be untouched. You would love God so much more deeply. You would care so much more about your brothers and sisters in Christ. And you would have such a passion for souls.

As we'll see later, the whole purpose of the Christian life is that God takes over more and more of our lives. That he molds his character in us. That we be conformed to the image of his son, Jesus Christ. That's what radical renewal is all about. But that isn't the experience of most Christians. And it isn't what the world sees when it looks at the majority of people in the church today. Many are still wandering in the desert.

When people look at you and me, what do they see? Do they see God in us? The nightmare that haunts me the most is a news reporter asking my wife and close friends, "What is Luis Palau really like?" and having them say, "He's a phony. He talks about the power of God, but I don't see any of it in his life." That would kill me.

Why? Because what really counts is this: Does God run my life? Is he in control? Or am I trying to run the show?

Do people see God in your life and in mine? Is every area of our lives dominated and filled with God himself? Painfully, the answer is sometimes no. I'll tell you the reason why.

WHY ARE WE MISSING OUT? 3

When Air Canada took delivery of four Boeing 767s several years ago, the new jumbo jets were the pride of the fleet. That is, until Flight 143 from Montreal to Edmonton one fateful Monday.

After a short hop from Montreal to Ottawa, Captain Robert Pearson and copilot Marcel Quintal maneuvered the plane back into the air for the 2,000-mile trip to Edmonton. Passengers were enjoying a movie when the jumbo jet's massive engines abruptly stopped.

Only those without earphones noticed at first. Then came a break in the movie. Captain Pearson announced that Flight 143 would be making an emergency landing. Sixty-nine people were trapped in an agonizingly slow but inescapable descent to earth.

For several minutes, a desperate silence hung over the cabin. Then fear gave way to screams as the crash landing neared. All the latest technology couldn't keep the jumbo jet in the air another second.

Eight hundred miles short of its destination, Flight 143 ran out of fuel. Anyone could have made the same mistake. The electronic digital fuel gauge on the Boeing 767 was out of order so, as the rules permit, Captain Pearson and copilot Quintal had relied on figures given by the refueling crew before takeoff.

But someone on the refueling crew confused pounds for

kilograms. Somewhere over Winnipeg the truth emerged. The jumbo jet should have had 26,760 pounds of fuel left. It had none.

By God's grace, Captain Pearson and copilot Quintal were able to glide Flight 143 some 100 miles to a former military air field Quintal remembered from his air force days. A dramatic crash landing heavily damaged the jumbo jet's landing gear, but no one on board was hurt.

Unfortunately, for others in life the landing is not always so happy.

A Desperate Situation

Thousands of Christians right now are in a desperate situation. They know it's possible to live a victorious and holy life, one filled with God himself. But they aren't living on that level. Instead, they're slowly gliding toward earth—weighed down with dissatisfaction, discouragement, and defeat. Their efforts to regain spiritual momentum have proven ineffective, and they're deathly afraid of what's next—a crash landing.

Why do we see so many spiritual disasters?

Why do we suffer so many unnecessary defeats?

Why so much depression?

Why so much carnality?

I've heard all kinds of excuses. If you're a counselor or small-group leader or deacon or elder or pastor, you've probably heard many of them, too. "Times are tough financially. It's hard to play it straight in the business world." Or, "With all the openness about sexuality these days, what am I supposed to do?" "I just don't love my wife anymore, so why should I stay with her?" "I know I should spend more time reading the Bible, but with the demands of work and all, well, I also need time just to relax."

People talk as if there is no way in today's world to walk in the light of God's Word, by his Spirit. "I want to be holy, really, but the media make it so tough. We live in such a sensual society. How can anyone stay pure anymore?"

Admittedly, the world is a very unholy place.

English journalist Malcolm Muggeridge said the crisis of our day isn't political or economic or ecological but "the loss of a sense of moral order." Reverend Richard Halverson says "moral, ethical anarchy" is ransacking our society. Relativism reigns supreme.

But even if we did live in a godly society, there would be other excuses. "If you knew my spouse, you wouldn't talk about the victorious Christian life. I invite you to be a guest at our house for a week, Luis, then tell me how victorious you feel." Or, "My mother-in-law is staying with us and until she goes home, believe me, there ain't no victory in our house." Or, "You don't know how tough it is in my job. I can't be honest and survive."

People can make any excuse they want, but let me say this with authority from God's Word: No one can take away the anointing of the Holy Spirit from our lives. No one can keep our cup from running over. No one can steal the joy of the Lord from us. Not our in-laws. Not our spouse. Not our boss. Not even Satan. No one! No matter how ugly they are or how big a pain they may be.

Only one thing can keep you and me from enjoying the Christian life to the fullest extent possible…

Sin.

There's nothing else to blame. This is the negative side of radical renewal, but we have to acquire a new vision of sin. We need to recognize sin for what it truly is…a deadly spiritual cancer within our souls.

If you and I want to experience all the tremendous possibilities of the Christian life, we can! The only thing that makes us bitter, or frustrated, or defeated, or ugly, or dark, or a pain to others, is sin.

Sin is a horrible subject. But unless we are completely right with God and have nothing to confess to him, you and I have to face this issue squarely. Solemnly, we need to speak the truth before the Lord.

The Need for Divine Surgery

If you took your spouse or best friend to the doctor because he or she had discovered a potentially cancerous growth, what would you expect the doctor to say? "Take two aspirin and call me in the morning"? No way! If he said that to me, I'd storm out and never come back. If the situation is serious, I want the doctor to tell me the truth. What is this lump? We need to know. If it's bad, we want it out.

My wife, Pat, and I actually faced this trial several years ago. Pat discovered a lump, so we immediately took her to the doctor. He determined the lump was cancerous, so radical surgery was scheduled for the next Monday. Then months (actually years) of recovery followed. But what if we'd ignored the doctor's findings and canceled the surgery? The consequences, almost certainly, would have been disastrous. Sure, the surgery and treatment were painful, but they were better than losing my wife.

No doctor gets pleasure from cutting into a patient in order to remove cancerous tissue. But it has to be done.

I feel the same way in dealing with the subject of sin. If you and I are living with any form of sin in our hearts, it's deadly.

Unless we undergo God's divine surgery, sin will grow ever more malignant. The Lord's work in and through us eventually will be squelched. We can't go on day after day, year after year as if nothing is wrong.

We begin by asking God to examine our hearts. Our prayer can be that of the psalmist: "Search me, O God, and know my heart; try me, and know my anxieties; and see if there is any wicked way in me (Psalm 139:23-24 NKJV).

It's not enough to pretend we're walking with the Lord. How sensitive are we to sin? Are we indulging in talk and activities that defile our soul? If so, we are grieving the Holy Spirit—even if we don't sense it. Sometimes it takes a while before we realize, "I have lost the joy. I used to be so happy in the Lord. What happened?"

We need to ask God to make us increasingly sensitive to sin. That's especially important in the culture in which we live today. Moral standards have been knocked down and kicked around. Ethics are now being decided by preference and public opinion.

In such days, I find this prayer of commitment incredibly relevant and challenging: "I will walk in my house with blameless heart. I will set before my eyes no vile thing. The deeds of faithless men I hate; they will not cling to me. Men of perverse heart shall be far from me; I will have nothing to do with evil" (Psalm 101:2-4).

Scripture says there must not be even a hint of immorality or impurity in our lives. We're to have no partnership with the ungodly, and nothing to do with the fruitless deeds of darkness (Ephesians 5:3-11).

What deeds of darkness are lodged within our souls? I tremble at the thought of even discussing this subject. I certainly can't point an accusing finger at you; I'm a sinner like everyone else. But I've experienced God's divine surgery, and I know how important it is to go through this process.

Pinpointing Any Unconfessed Sins

The secret of ongoing, continuous renewal is brokenness and repentance. You and I humbly need to ask the Holy Spirit to search our hearts repeatedly. Is my conscience clear right now, or is it contaminated? Do I need to admit any weaknesses or failures?

This process of examination takes more than a moment's reflection, but can begin at any time. It may take place under the preaching of God's Word next Sunday. It can start while we're quietly reading the Bible tomorrow morning. The process may even begin before we're finished with this chapter. I know God wants to speak to my heart as I write about this subject. Ask him to speak to you as you continue reading.

When God does begin to speak to us, the temptation is to

think immediately of someone else. If a sermon gets too convicting, we say to ourselves, "I hope Mrs. Smith is listening right now!" Or we begin to read something powerful but then give it to someone else to take the pressure off us. Rather than thinking about others who need this message, let's ask God to speak to our hearts right now during the next few minutes.

Drifting into Moral Indifference

Christians never fall into gross sin overnight. The Lord doesn't allow that. Don't worry that somehow you're going to be walking along and then—boom!—Satan is going to drag you off into some terrible sin.

Sin usually encroaches an inch at a time. One minor disobedience because of a lack of dedication and surrender eventually leads to other things. C. S. Lewis said that our big choices for good or evil are conditioned by "private little choices" made along the way.

Those private little choices can end up redirecting the whole course of our lives. People who shipwreck their lives never intended to steer so far off course. But little deceptions here, little white lies there, tiny things along the way lowered their moral and spiritual sensitivity and sent them drifting.

Let's think about the private little choices we've made. Have you begun to drift into a sea of indifference without realizing it?

Please don't gloss over the next few pages. Instead, ask God to search your heart as you think through some common areas of compromise.

Becoming Absorbed with Self

Today everybody's talking about self-acceptance, self-actualization, self-advancement, self-affirmation, self-awareness, self-esteem, self-fulfillment, self-gratification, self-image, self-importance, self-improvement, self-perception, self-satisfaction, self-sufficiency, self-understanding, self-worth.

Of course you recognize the common denominator in all these. Yet what is the greatest enemy of the fullness of the Spirit? Self!

Our culture subscribes to the cult of self. We're bombarded by its propaganda through newspaper and magazine articles, radio and television programs, and endless advertisements.

The world talks about self all the time, and it's easy for us to talk this way, too.

Recently I heard about a pastor's wife who went to an aerobic dance class to lose a little weight, be herself, and all that. The place was jammed with divorced women who complained that men are "a bunch of pigs," "indifferent," and "unfulfilling." And this woman, a pastor's wife, bought into it, and eventually

walked out on her husband. Why? Primarily because she became completely focused on self.

You and I can fall into the same trap. We can justify our
absorption with self. We can explain it away. We can use any
argument we want, but it's destroying marriages and homes.
It's needlessly diverting people from true meaning and purpose
in life.

Repeating Gossip

Perhaps you're thinking, "Come on, Luis. Deal with some of
the big sins." This is a heavy one. Most of us are not about to
commit adultery—if nothing else, out of fear of God. But what
hurts Christian families and congregations more than almost
anything else? People who gossip, saying things that shouldn't
be repeated.

Gossip isn't telling a lie about someone else. That's slander.
Gossip is when we learn something that's probably true about
someone and we repeat it when we know we shouldn't. We all
have this tendency. People love to pull it out of us, and we love
to draw it out of others.

Some people are magnets for gossip. They know things the
FBI hasn't discovered. You might be friends with someone
like that, and every time you talk to that person you end up
feeling dirty.

It's tough to stop someone from telling us all that garbage, isn't it? It's even harder to forget it instead of passing it on. But Scripture says to get rid of this sin. Don't accept it or excuse it! This, too, has to be confessed.

Harboring Unbelief

This may be the most serious and devastating sin of all. If we're cynical, we wouldn't dare admit unbelief to our parents or spouse or children. But in our hearts, we sit back and question what the Word of God clearly teaches. What dishonor this brings to the Lord!

Take the Lord's command to "seek first his [God's] kingdom and his righteousness" and his promise that "all these things [material needs] will be given to you as well" (Matthew 6:33). This is one of my favorite verses. I believe it. I know it's true and for more than 40 years my life has proven it. Nevertheless, how many times have I despaired over financial or other needs? The Lord has never failed me, but I still sometimes panic and distrust him. That's committing the sin of unbelief.

Or take the promise that "sin shall not have dominion over you, for you are not under law but under grace" (Romans 6:14 NKJV). Now someone can argue that verse isn't a promise, or that only pietists and "holiness" folks believe it. That's an insult to God. It's like having your best friend mention she is buying you a terrific gift only to have you snarl back, "Forget it. That's

ridiculous. I don't believe you for a second. You have no intention of getting me any such gift." You might be right after a
response like that. Your friend would be hurt and upset at you,
and properly so.

Do we insult God the same way by refusing to believe his
promises throughout scripture?

Is there cynicism in your soul? Is there contempt for the
clear-cut, revealed promises of God? Do you hear about the
possibilities of the Christian life and say, "Sure, go ahead, talk
about it all you want. But I know better"? Bring that unbelief to
Jesus today.

Maintaining an Unthankful Spirit

Although many of us enjoy material blessings, it's so easy to
complain about what we don't have instead of praising God for
all the good things he has given to us.

Many years ago when my wife and I were preparing to be missionaries, our salary was a few hundred dollars a month. It
definitely didn't seem like enough for a missionary family of
four. But we were rejoicing the Lord was providing for all of
our needs. Another missionary heard my praise and snapped,
"Come on, Luis. You're from South America, so anything is a
big deal to you. But I was born in the United States, and this is
not enough money for a guy to survive."

I kept my mouth shut, but I never forgot that fellow's remarks. Today he's divorced and chasing his own dreams instead of serving God. He was a thankless Christian. Instead of saying, "Lord, thank you that I'm healthy; I have food to eat; I've got clothes to wear," he complained about what he didn't have.

I believe thanklessness is a great sin against the Lord. Maybe you haven't succeeded like you thought you were going to when you entered the work world. Maybe you're having a rough time of it at home. But if you forget to thank God for his goodness to you, even in the midst of your problems, you grieve him. You suffocate the Holy Spirit's work in your life and you keep yourself from his further blessing.

Feeling Resentful

Because our culture has almost made materialism a religion, it's extremely easy to become resentful. My grandparents were from Europe, but I happened to grow up in Argentina. My family became fairly well off, thanks to my dad's hard work, wise planning, and the blessing of the Lord on his life.

Then my dad died unexpectedly at the age of 35. Within three years our family was living in poverty, to the point where we couldn't pay our rent for eight months. It was only the mercy of our landlord that kept us from being thrown out on the street.

Despite our poverty, my mother never became resentful. She

almost made a point of saying "Isn't that exciting?" whenever we heard about someone going on a vacation or buying something expensive. She never complained: "Why, they know I'm a widow with six children. They should know we're destitute. Why don't they give us the money instead?"

My mother taught us never to become resentful toward others. Some nights she had nothing more than a loaf of French bread with a little garlic to serve seven people for dinner. Yet my mother always rejoiced, and she gladly celebrated with others. Her attitude was a fantastic example to me.

Scripture doesn't just say "mourn with those who mourn" but also "rejoice with those who rejoice" (Romans 12:15). Resentment is an awful sin. Even out of enlightened self-interest, it's best to rejoice. Resentment only makes you dislikable. So rejoice with those who rejoice. Do it because the Lord says so and because it's the godly thing to do. Get into the habit of rejoicing with others out loud, especially if you feel a tinge of resentment.

Making Petty Complaints

I have seen many revivals during more than 30 years of ministry. My first was at a church in Colombia where I was serving as a missionary-evangelist. That revival was nearly destroyed by a petty complaint.

Two weeks into the revival, one of the church elders stood to speak during a service. Apparently there had been a mix-up. This elder had spent the equivalent of ten dollars on flowers, but someone else's flowers were used to decorate the pulpit area instead.

"This isn't fair," the elder complained. "It was my turn to buy the flowers. What about all the money I've just spent?" He said this in front of everyone, including dozens of new believers. That single attitude over something irrelevant and forgettable stirred up needless trouble and almost ruined the meeting.

Often it's the little things that kill the joy of the Lord among us. A series of little things left unconfessed and accumulated can devastate us and those around us.

Before my wife and I left for our first missionary term overseas, our mission board sent us to visit a church in California. It held a business meeting that Sunday night. We were sitting on one side of the church. The pastor and his fretful wife were seated up front. You could sense trouble.

As the meeting started, someone stood and said, "I feel that our pastor. ..." and laid out her complaint. Then a man got up and said, "I agree with Mrs. Smith. The pastor has done this and that." The pastor hadn't committed sin. They were complaining about petty things, but they made a big deal out of it.

Suddenly a teenage girl in the back stood up and began to cry.

"What are you people doing? Why are you trying to hurt my dad? He's a wonderful man. He loves you all. He prays for you every morning. I've heard him cry for you in his office. Why are you saying all these things about him?"

How wicked Christians can be. The things we say about others. Of course they make mistakes, but don't we all? How can we be so wicked?

Neglecting to Tithe

It's estimated that only a small percentage of the Christians in this country give to local evangelism and overseas missions. Up to 85 percent are indifferent to the Great Commission. That's incredible when you think how much God has blessed us materially and spiritually.

We miss out on the further blessing of God when we neglect to give to evangelism, missions, and the ongoing ministry of our local church. Jesus said, "Give, and it will be given to you. A good measure, pressed down, shaken together and running over, will be poured into your lap. For with the measure you use, it will be measured to you" (Luke 6:38). We're to give ourselves 100 percent to the Lord, then give generously and cheerfully from our substance.

When my wife and I were serving in Latin America, my giving tended to be spontaneous and, therefore, sporadic. If I saw or heard about a need, I would respond "as the Lord leads." Then the Lord taught me the joy of giving regularly and sacrificially. I feel truly blessed now when I give to my local church and when I send gifts to people serving the Lord in various parts of the world. It's a fantastic joy. Is that your experience yet? Or is this an area you need to confess to the Lord?

Ignoring Recurring Sins

Some people have no problem enjoying victory over the temptation to lie or lose their temper, but they struggle with lust. Lust has become a recurring sin in their life. For others, their recurring sin may be covetousness, envy, jealousy, or some other vice.

We all have at least one recurring sin, a sin that keeps tripping us up (Hebrews 12:1). We can end up feeling almost obsessed by it. "Why can't I defeat this sin?" we ask.

"Why does this particular temptation always plague me?" Satan attacks us in other areas, of course, but we shouldn't be surprised he concentrates on our area of weakness.

For our spiritual health and well-being, it's critical that we identify our recurring sin by name. We don't want to reinforce such sin by always talking about it or thinking about it. But until we name our recurring sin, and take necessary steps to overcome it (which I'll talk about later), we'll continue giving in to it and feeling more and more frustrated and defeated.

What is your recurring sin? Have you confessed it to the Lord? Have you made a list of realistic steps to take to avoid it in the future? Have you asked a spiritually mature Christian friend to keep you accountable? Are you actively avoiding places of temptation? Are you on your guard against pride after each victory?

Beware of falling into the snare of thinking, "I've gone too far. I'm trapped. I'll never have victory over this sin again." As we'll see in chapter 6, God's power at work within you can completely liberate you from any and all sin.

I've seen God liberate alcoholics, prostitutes, cold-blooded murderers, and little old ladies with dirty rotten attitudes by the power of the gospel and the reality that "Jesus lives in me." He can do the same in your life!

Lacking True Joy

Do you lack a genuine sense of joy? Yes, that's a sin, too. We're commanded to "Rejoice in the Lord always. I will say it again: Rejoice!" (Philippians 4:4). Yet a lack of joy often marks our lives as Christians. Years ago, I had to identify the lack of joy for what it is—one of my recurring sins.

God doesn't want us to be flighty, shallow clowns with silly grins painted on our faces. Clowns are all right for circuses, but God commands us to be genuinely joyful day in and day out.

That doesn't mean we don't experience trials and hardships. But in the midst of those trials and hardships, we can rejoice. After all, the apostle Paul wrote his commands to "rejoice!" while locked away in a Roman jail.

Some people have remarked, "I may not look happy on the outside, but deep down inside I have great joy." Sometimes that's hard to swallow. There should be evidence of such joy. I don't believe there's a difference between true happiness and joy, though you may disagree with me on that point.

Engaging in Sexual Impurity

This is a delicate subject, but if we don't face this issue, it can destroy us. King David learned this the hard way by committing adultery with the wife of one of his most trustworthy men and then having that military leader killed. David paid the consequences for the rest of his life. But I believe David's problem began long before that act of adultery, when he was young.

David never dealt with this issue before the Lord. David talked to God about whether to go to war against the Philistines or refrain from battle. He cried out to God in his distress and he praised God for his goodness. As far as I can tell, David prayed about almost every area except sexual temptation, which happened to be one of his areas of recurring sin. He ended up an embarrassed old man when he could have finished victoriously.

I'm long into the Christian life now and I've probably seen it all. But today there is a duplicity when it comes to sexuality. Instead of holding to God's standard of purity, professing Christians are committing fornication, adultery, even homosexuality. It's bad enough such things are happening, but some Christians are even trying to justify their sinful behavior.

What God forbids and says he hates, we often hear discussed with such lightheartedness that it shocks the world and shakes the younger generation in our churches. And then we wonder why there's no blessing. Why there's no power. Why there's no joy. Why there's no victory. Why there's no revival and renewal. It's because there is no holiness. I hate to talk about this, but we can't ignore reality.

I think men may have it just a bit rougher than most women when it comes to dealing with sexual temptation. Are you tempted to thumb through magazines with suggestive or pornographic pictures? Are you tempted to watch immorality on the screen? If you're giving in to such temptation, go to the Lord and confess your sins now.

I've seen friends, including some in the ministry, destroy themselves. And I've helped counsel countless others who have experienced grief caused by immorality and infidelity.

The Bible says those who are committed to Jesus have crucified the flesh with its passions and desires (Galatians 5:24). God wants us to deal radically and ruthlessly with sin. There's no room for pampering or playing around.

Hanging on to Bitterness

A friend of mine went through a massive emotional breakdown. After his recovery, we went for a walk. "Luis," he told me, "don't allow anyone to ever make you bitter."

He told me about his breakdown—running down the street naked, weird stuff.

"My problems began when I got so worked up about the contractor who didn't build my basement and driveway right. I hated what he'd done to my home. And since he lived next door, I saw him almost daily. Each time I saw him, my anger and bitterness grew even more intense until I finally cracked!"

No wonder God's Word is so emphatic: "Get rid of all bitterness" (Ephesians 4:31). Why? Because if a "bitter root grows up" within you, it will "cause trouble and defile many" (Hebrews 12:15).

Not everybody breaks down emotionally from unresolved bitterness, but I've met many people who have allowed it to poison their lives. A young woman came up to me in Scotland after I had preached about parent-child relationships.

"I can't obey my father!" she said. "He's gone to Saudi Arabia for three years. He never comes home. I refuse to honor and obey him." She was clearly angry and bitter. After we'd talked, I said, "Look, the Bible says honor and obey your father, whether you feel like it or not." I advised her to write to her father and honestly say how hurt she felt he didn't come home or write or call very often. I also urged her to confess her bitterness, then tell her father that she would honor and obey him from now on in obedience to God's Word.

Several months later I received a note from this young Scottish woman. "I've never felt so free as when I followed your advice and wrote that letter. In fact, because of that letter, my father did come home. He asked forgiveness from my mother and me, and our family is reconciled once again!"

What happens if we don't deal with bitterness in our soul? Eventually, we become bitter at God himself. This is one of the most shocking sins imaginable. People actually shake their fists and angrily shout, "God, why did you let this happen?"

When my wife got cancer, we told people there are two ways of asking *why*. There is the bitter, defiant *why*, and there is the intelligent, understanding *why*. One is blasphemy. The other is an appropriate, Christian response to the hardships of life.

Many times I prayed while my wife was going through all the rigors of surgery and chemotherapy: "Why is this happening, Lord? What am I supposed to learn from this? Is there any reason why it happened? Is there anything that we as a family need to learn? Is there anything I need to be able to learn to minister to others more effectively?"

That's completely different from, "God, I'm mad at you. Why the hell did you allow my wife to come down with cancer? We've got four boys...."

Such outbursts reveal a bitter heart.

We must deal decisively with such anger.

Some Christian counselors and psychologists have suggested that people vent their angry feelings toward God. Since when is God to blame? Yet this form of blasphemy is being justified in numerous articles and books.

That doesn't make it any less a sin.

If your father was wicked to you and you've hated him for 20 years, don't blame God. And don't remain bitter against your father, either. Someone might say, "Well, that's easy for you to say, Luis. You probably had a great dad." Thank God, I did. And I have a wonderful wife, too. But I've had other things done to me. Vicious criticisms and attacks. Unjust accusations from the enemies of the gospel. People have tried to destroy me and my ministry in certain countries. It hurts. By nature, I want to hit back. It's not fair. But the minute I get angry and bitter, I grieve the Holy Spirit.

If you're bitter against someone, or angry at God, don't play games. Ask God to perform divine surgery. Get on your knees beside your bed or wherever you can pray alone and confess your bitterness by name. Tell the whole story to the Lord. Yes, the Lord already knows all the details, but confess it anyway. Admit your sins to him.

Clearing the Slate

It's time to do business with God. Ask the Lord to search your heart right now. Get alone and take a sheet of notebook paper and pen. (I'm serious. Do this.)

On the top left-hand side of your sheet write: "Things I must get right with God this week:" On the top right-hand side: "Things I must clear up with other people:"

In the left-hand column, write down any sins God shows you. We've considered only a few in this chapter. We could have picked a hundred others that Scripture addresses: impatience, worry, pride, self-righteousness, independence, laziness, greed, substance abuse, carelessness, divisiveness, disloyalty, demandingness, prayerlessness, neglect of the Lord's Supper, lack of commitment to the local church, or whatever.

Ask God to do a deep work in your soul. Write down every sin you're guilty of, whether it takes half a sheet of paper or half a dozen pages. Don't rush. Don't assume you don't have any unconfessed sins. Why let them keep piling up because you're always in a hurry? Take time out to be quiet before the Lord, away from distractions. Allow him to examine every area of your life. If you're serious, he won't hesitate to convict you of specific sins.

As you list your sins, in the right-hand column write the names of anyone you've hurt, deceived, been bitter against, gossiped about, failed to show love and compassion to, you've cheated, or whatever the offense might be.

If you're young, perhaps you improperly broke off a friendship or dating relationship. You hurt that person but have never asked for forgiveness. Or maybe your relationship with a parent, sibling, or your spouse is strained. Have you admitted what you've done wrong? Are you actively seeking reconciliation? Have you forgiven them even if they won't be reconciled to you?

Is there someone to whom you owe restitution? Perhaps you've cheated in a business deal or let a debt go bad. Like Zacchaeus the tax collector, maybe you've taken advantage of people. Are you willing to break that cycle of sin? Do you want to make things right?

A university student told me, "Luis, if I listed everything, I figure I'd have to write down about 500 things." So I asked him, "What's the biggest thing you've done you need to make right?" He admitted that one night after a football game in high school, he and three friends blew up a gas station and destroyed three cars.

I told this young man that he had to confess this to God, then go and make restitution. "I could never pay for that," he objected, but he already was paying for it…inside. He had become suicidal. Sin was eating away at his soul.

We can't afford to delay God's divine surgery in our lives. Even if surgery is painful, the cancer of sin never stops growing. So take time now before the Lord and let him speak to your heart. Write down any known sins, and ask God to reveal your hidden faults. Write them all down, but don't put your name on the list or leave it around for anyone else to see.

As you write out your list of items to clear up with the Lord and with other people, there's no need to be weighed down by undefined guilt. The Holy Spirit who indwells us will clearly pinpoint the sins we've committed.

Satan accuses, but the Spirit convicts. If you feel a vague sense of guilt but can't put your finger on a particular sin, that guilt probably is not from the Lord. Ask, "God, is this sense of guilt from you? If so, please make clear what I've done wrong." The Holy Spirit doesn't accuse us, condemn us, or lay a cloud of guilt and depression over us. If we spend time quietly before the Lord, he will convict us of the specific sins we have committed.

Taking time to listen to the Lord and write down our sins is a crucial first step toward radical renewal and getting out of the desert. We're suddenly at a point of crisis. We have to make a choice. Proverbs 28:13 says, "He who conceals his transgressions will not prosper, but he who confesses and forsakes them will obtain mercy" (RSV). We can choose to cover up our sins and reap the consequences. Or we can confess them and allow God to do a good work in our soul.

I urge you to do business with God without delay. In his presence, confess every sin the Holy Spirit brings to mind. You don't have to dredge up old sins that already have been forgiven. But ask the Lord to "cleanse me from secret faults" (Psalm 19:12 NKJV).

Are you willing to do it? Are you ready? I hope so. Even if you've asked God to search your heart before, ask him now… again. Write out your list.

Next, we'll consider what to do with it.

NOT UNTIL YOU'RE CLEAN 4

As with many cities, the skyline where I live in Portland has changed dramatically during the past few decades. One of the most prominent features now is the Oregon Convention Center with twin towers stretching 260 feet above the massive complex.

Shortly before the center was completed, however, its impressive jade-green glass towers suddenly posed a problem that threatened to delay the opening of the $90 million project. Apparently, back in the design stages, no one stopped long enough to ask, "How is anybody going to clean these glass towers?" It wasn't until construction was well under way that someone recognized the problem. Standard window-washing systems couldn't handle the job. So a Los Angeles-based engineering firm was hired to figure out a way to keep the twin spires from becoming permanently dirty and discolored.

Thankfully, God thought about the problem of cleansing our hearts long before he created Adam and Eve. And he knew exactly what he was going to do to cleanse us thoroughly, even though the drama of redemption wasn't played out in human history for several thousand years.

"It was just before the Passover Feast. Jesus knew that the time had come for him to leave this world and go to the Father. Having loved his own who were in the world, he now showed them the full extent of his love.

"The evening meal was being served, and the devil had already prompted Judas Iscariot, son of Simon, to betray Jesus. Jesus knew the Father had put all things under his power, and that he had come from God and was returning to God; so he got up from the meal, took off his outer clothing, and wrapped a towel around his waist. After that, he poured water into a basin and began to wash his disciples' feet, drying them with the towel that was wrapped around him.

"He came to Simon Peter, who said to him, 'Lord, are you going to wash my feet?'

"Jesus replied, 'You do not realize now what I am doing, but later you will understand.'

"'No,' said Peter, 'you shall never wash my feet.'

"Jesus answered, 'Unless I wash you, you have no part with me.'

"'Then, Lord,' Simon Peter replied, 'not just my feet but my hands and my head as well.'

"Jesus answered, 'A person who has had a bath needs only to wash his feet; his whole body is clean. And you are clean, though not every one of you!' For he knew who was going to betray him, and that was why he said not everyone was clean.

"When he had finished washing their feet, he put on his clothes and returned to his place. 'Do you understand what I have done for you?' he asked them. 'You call me Teacher and Lord, and rightly so, for that is what I am. Now that I, your Lord and Teacher, have washed your feet, you also should wash one another's feet. I have set you an example that you should do as I have done for you. I tell you the truth, no servant is greater than his master, nor is a messenger greater than the one who sent him. Now that you know these things, you will be blessed if you do them'" (John 13:1-17).

Acknowledging Our Defilement

In New Testament times, people ate an evening meal while reclining on a couch or cushions on the floor around a low table. Before sitting down, however, everybody removed their sandals. Naturally, it wasn't very pleasant for others if you had dirty feet.

The guests may have taken a bath before coming. But then they had to walk along dusty and dirty roads. Most streets were filled with a wide assortment of people and animals. Often city streets were littered with garbage and refuse. So the host of the meal normally would have a servant or slave wash the feet of each guest and dry them with a towel. It was a disagreeable job, but it had to be done. Then the guests would walk into the dining area, visit with the host, and enjoy a pleasant meal together.

On this particular occasion, however, Jesus and his disciples were borrowing a room to eat their final Passover meal together. They had no servants and none of the disciples had thought about bringing a basin, towel, and pitcher of water to wash everyone else's feet. Only Jesus thought about it. Why? Because he "did not come to be served, but to serve, and to give his life as a ransom for many" (Mark 10:45).

Try to picture this scene. Even though Jesus knows his death is imminent, he does the work of a slave. The Master himself. The Son of God. The Creator of heaven and earth.

He gets on his knees.

The disciples should have washed his feet, but Jesus kneels down and washes the feet of one of his disciples, then dries them with the towel wrapped around his waist. He then kneels by another disciple and washes his feet. Jesus keeps going around the room until he reaches Peter.

Suddenly the scene focuses on this one apostle. Peter was one of the Lord's most prominent disciples. Whenever Jesus healed someone away from the crowds, Peter was there. When Jesus invited his closest disciples to witness his transfiguration, Peter was there. Peter stood out among the disciples. He was a leader with a tremendous zeal for the Lord. As a spokesman for the group, he was the first to declare his belief in Jesus as the Messiah, the Christ, the unique Son of God. But Peter was also fallible. He tended to be rash, and his impulsive statements got him into trouble more than once.

When Jesus knelt to wash Peter's feet, Peter couldn't contain himself. "What? Are you going to wash my feet?" The other disciples were paralyzed, astonished that their Master would take the place of a slave. But Peter, with his big mouth, wouldn't let Jesus do it. The atmosphere in the Upper Room must have become electric.

Now, everyone in that Upper Room had come in with defiled and dirty feet. Just walking half a mile down the dusty, dirty streets of Jerusalem would have contaminated them. It didn't matter how recently they'd had a bath. Everyone had polluted feet. Everyone needed to have his feet cleansed.

Similarly, you and I often become defiled as we walk through this world. Even if we're trying to please God in everything we do and say, we still hear things we don't want to hear. We see things we didn't intend to see. We're defiled just going to the supermarket and coming straight home.

Many Christians work in offices or factories with men and women whose language and stories color our thinking. It doesn't matter if we read Scripture, memorize key verses, spend time in prayer and sing choruses of praise to the Lord before going to work each day. Our mind is still polluted by the filth we hear.

Or maybe you work with people who dress suggestively or who make passes at fellow employees and customers. You can't be around them long before you get polluted.

If we want to break free from the desert and be radically renewed, we need to be honest enough to admit, "Lord Jesus, I've been defiled as I've walked through this fallen world. I want to sit at the table of fellowship with you and with my brothers and sisters in Christ. But there's no way I want to sit there with dirty, polluted feet."

That's the picture I see in the Upper Room. The disciples had arrived with dirty feet, so the Lord humbles himself and begins to wash their feet. Then Peter exposes his defiant heart.

Recognizing Our Defiance

Peter's dusty feet symbolized a deeper problem, only he wouldn't admit it. At first it sounds like Peter is being humble. But if you listen again, you can almost hear the pride and arrogance when Peter says, "You will never wash my feet, Lord."

What a contradiction! Peter wasn't saying this to one of the other disciples. He's talking to Jesus, the Messiah, the Savior, the King of kings and Lord of lords.

But Peter's defiance doesn't catch Jesus off guard. Jesus quietly and patiently and lovingly gives Peter the shock treatment.

"All right, Peter. You don't want Me to wash your feet? Fine. But if I don't wash your feet, you can have no part with Me."

The Lord does the same thing with us. We put up a front and pretend we're okay the way we are. But in our hearts the Lord is making it very clear: "You can have no part with Me until I wash you."

No part in service.

No part in worship.

No part in fellowship.

We can go to church and sing the songs and raise our hands. But the Lord still says, "If I don't wash you, you can have no part with me."

That's where an incredible number of Christians are stuck today. Older men and women, even pastors and their spouses, have never progressed beyond this point—they've never been thoroughly cleansed from sin. As a result, they have never begun to experience God's renewal in their lives.

It's hard to think someone could be a child of God and yet have a miserable, frustrated life. But if sin is in their heart—they can have it no other way. Again and again the Lord has said, "Please let me wash your feet." Yet, we keep saying no. So the Lord responds, "Well, then, you can't have any part with Me."

The Lord uses strong words to slay Peter's pride. If Peter didn't permit the Lord to cleanse him from daily defilement, from the impurities of mind, heart, and soul that accumulated as he went through the world, he could have no part in fellowship with Jesus.

Jesus' strong words are meant for you and me, too.

You may be a pastor. You may be an executive or professional. You may be a university professor or student. Whatever your situation in life, if you're a Christian, then Jesus is saying to you, and saying to me, "Let Me wash your feet. If I don't, you can have no part with Me."

We can't pretend to walk in the light with God if we have polluted ourselves. Without that regular cleansing, we're still children of God, but we have no fellowship. No joy. No power. We're incapable of serving the living God (Hebrews 9:14). He can't use us.

Just as people in the first century had to wash their feet repeatedly, we too must have our spiritual feet washed day after day. Otherwise, we lose God's blessing on our life and ministry.

God is a God of love. That's why he's at our feet, ready to wash them. But God is also just, and the two go together. You can't separate God's love from his justice. Therefore, it's ridiculous to think we can sin all we want "and the God of love is going to have to forgive me." Really? What makes us think we're going to get away with that attitude?

The New Testament commands us not to play games with God. "Do not be deceived. God cannot be mocked. A man reaps what he sows. The one who sows to please his sinful nature, from that nature will reap destruction; the one who sows to please the Spirit, from the Spirit will reap eternal life" (Galatians 6:7-8).

As far as you know, is everything right between you and your heavenly Father? Is everything clear between you and others? In other words, do you have clean feet?

Admitting Our Desperation

This shock treatment finally woke up Peter to his desperate condition. He finally cries out, "Master, not my feet only! Wash my hands, wash my head. Pour it on. Do the whole job."

Peter may have had a big mouth, but he had a quick brain and a good heart. To have no part with Jesus was intolerable to Peter. So Peter said, in essence, "Lord, please don't toss me on the sidelines. Don't put me on the shelf. Don't file me away."

The very thought horrified Peter. It's horrifying to imagine it happening to you and me. But if we refuse to be cleansed day by day, we will end up in the grandstands watching the game but never playing. We'll be on the bookshelf and never be read. We'll be filed away like some old forgotten memo and never seen or used again. What an awful thought!

How does the Lord respond to Peter? "Don't go overboard now, Peter. Listen, you've already had a spiritual shower the day you trusted in me. He who is bathed needs only to wash his feet."

That's true in our lives, too. When we became Christians, all our sins were forgiven. We were washed in the blood of Jesus Christ. We had a spiritual bath. It's what the Bible calls salvation.

But as we walk through this world, our feet become defiled. Sometimes we even become defiant, deliberately stepping into a mess by disobeying the Lord. And once again, we need to come to Jesus and allow him to wash our feet.

The Master is here, calling for you. He's kneeling at your feet, saying, "Take off your shoes. Let me wash your feet. You've picked up some of the dirt of this world. Let me wash you."

The Lord can wash us. He is more than capable. When he hung on the cross he took all our defilement and defiance on himself.

"He himself bore our sins in his body on the tree, so that we might die to sins and live for righteousness; by his wounds you have been healed" (1 Peter 2:24).

"God made him who had no sin to be sin for us, so that

in him we might become the righteousness of God"
(2 Corinthians 5:21).

"Christ died for sins once for all, the righteous for the unrigh-
teous, to bring you to God" (1 Peter 3:18).

Have you lost the joy of the Lord? Have you lost your power?
Have you lost your assurance? Come and get it! Don't wait
another day. Go to the Lord and say, "Master, you've seen my
list of sins. You know everything I've done. Please wash me,
cleanse me, purify me. I want to love you and serve you with
all my heart."

Do that and you can claim this wonderful promise from
God's Word:

"But if we walk in the light, as he [God] is in the light, we have
fellowship with one another, and the blood of Jesus, his Son,
cleanses us from all sin" (1 John 1:7).

You and I need to ask, "What have I done to hurt the Lord and
his people?" Let's humbly confess our sins before the Lord
and ask him to wash us. Then let's go and clear up things with
the people we've hurt or offended.

Don't say, "I've already had my feet washed by the Master. I
don't have to apologize to anyone." If you and I are broken
about our sin, we will clear the decks with other people. We

will pay back what we've stolen. We'll be completely washed and freed from guilt.

What does the Bible say?

"If we confess our sins, he [God] is faithful and just and will forgive us our sins and purify us from all unrighteousness" (1 John 1:9). Not just from the little sins, but from all unrighteousness. What a word of forgiveness to claim!

You may be thinking, "But Luis, I've committed a big sin. I mean, one of the big ones. Will God cleanse me from that?" Yes, if you confess your sin.

What Is Confession?

Confession is simply stating what you've done. If a crook were confessing a crime he committed, he would tell the policeman or judge, "Yes, I stole the goods. Yes, I pulled the trigger. Yes, I ran the light and smashed into the old lady's cat. I did it." That's confession. If you begin to say, "Well, you have to understand. I didn't mean to kill anyone. I was just playing with the gun." That's making excuses or outright lying.

Biblical confession means telling the Lord what you know you've done wrong, even if you've confessed that same type of sin many times before and you're ashamed to have to bring it up once more. Confession means admitting your recurring sins and acts of defiance. It even means saying, "Lord, there may be some secret sins I'm not aware of yet." The Lord will gladly wash you and eventually point out those hidden sins, too.

The first step toward radical renewal, as we saw in the last chapter, is to acknowledge our sins. That's confession. Perhaps you wrote down only one or two things. Maybe you have quite a lengthy list.

Now let's take the second step. Across your sheet of paper, write the words of three verses. Personalize them and make them your own.

- 1 John 1:7 – "The blood of Jesus cleanses me from all sin."

- 1 John 1:9 – "God forgives my sins and purifies me from all unrighteousness."

- Hebrews 10:17 – "My sins and lawless acts God will remember no more."

Have you written those verses across your list? I've done this and I urge you to do it, too. Then if it expresses what's on your heart, I invite you to pray this prayer of confession and cleansing to the Lord:

Lord, it's hard to believe you would be at my feet, but there you are. Please wash me. I've sinned against you. I've done

*things I shouldn't have done. And I have left undone things
I should have done. I am unworthy of your forgiveness. But
thank you for your blood, which cleanses me from all sin and
unrighteousness.*

*Now, Lord, help me to make restitution to those against whom
I have sinned. Give me grace with the people I need to talk
with; may they accept my apology. Help me to forgive those
who have spoken evil against me or in some other way hurt
me. Holy Spirit, help me never to think about those offenses
again. I want to be holy, free, joyful in you.*

When we confess our sins to the Lord, they're washed.
They're cleansed. "As far as the east is from the west, so far
has he [God] removed our transgressions from us" (Psalm
103:12). The Lord has hurled "all our iniquities into the depths
of the sea" (Micah 7:19). As Corrie ten Boom used to say, "The
Lord takes our sins and casts them to the bottom of the sea.
Then he puts out a little sign that says, 'No fishing allowed.'"

The Lord doesn't remember our sins anymore, and he doesn't
want us bringing them up again, either.

I urge you to look at your list and take care of anything you
need to clear up with someone else. Do it quickly, in person or
over the phone if necessary.

I know this step isn't easy. Sometimes the hardest people to
face are those in our immediate family. At one point when my

kids were young I felt there was something between me and one of my twins, Keith. So I talked with him and asked, "Keith, have I done anything that really hurt your feelings?"

Instantly, Keith said, "Yes."

I thought, *Oh, boy. What did I do that is still in the forefront of his thinking?*

Keith told me: "Last Christmas you promised to give me a certain toy and you never gave it to me."

The fact is, I'd completely forgotten about it. I probed further: "Is there anything else I've done that wasn't right and I've never asked for your forgiveness?"

Again, instantly, Keith said, "Yes!"

"And what was that?"

"You remember when Stephen was born?" Of course I remembered. We were living in Mexico City at the time. "When Mom said you had to go to the hospital because Stephen was going to be born, you left us at home and took off in a hurry. Remember?"

I remembered.

"Well, you took off, you left Mom at the hospital, and you forgot the suitcase with all the stuff." I couldn't believe all the details he recalled! "So you came back and you were real huffy. When you got here, the suitcase had been opened and everything was thrown all over the place. And you spanked me."

My heart sank.

"And you didn't do it?" I asked.

"No, I didn't."

I felt terrible. I hugged Keith and asked him to forgive me for my actions. That time of confession and forgiveness instantly improved our relationship.

That went so well that I called in Keith's twin brother, Kevin. After all, maybe I'd hurt him, too. "Have I ever done something wrong and never asked your forgiveness or promised you something and never fulfilled it?" I asked.

Without any hesitation, Kevin said, "Yes."

"What was it?"

"Last Christmas you promised us a certain toy and you never bought it for us." He had no idea I'd just talked to Keith about the same thing. Naturally, I took my sons to the store that day and bought that certain toy for the boys.

The important thing wasn't the toy. I probably wasn't paying attention when I made that promise. I shouldn't have made that promise so lightly. But I did, and I had to clear the decks with my boys.

If you suspect there's something between you and someone else, add that person's name to your list and talk to him. Humbly ask if you've done something to hurt or disappoint him. And be prepared to ask for his forgiveness and make things right.

Talk to one person at a time. Don't confess something you've done wrong to anyone other than the individual you've wronged. Dealing with such matters in a group setting can be damaging. Wait until you can talk privately.

This may take time, but clear the decks with each person you've hurt or offended. Then take your list and tear it up with thanksgiving and a song of praise to the Lord. Don't keep it around to remind you of your past sins. They're gone forever. What a sense of forgiveness and relief!

But the Lord doesn't stop there.

Washing One Another's Feet

Do you remember what Jesus said after he washed the disciples' feet? "Now that I, your Lord and teacher, have washed your feet, you also should wash one another's feet. I have set you an example that you should do as I have done for you.... Now that you know these things, you will be blessed if you do them" (John 13:14-17).

Jesus had just washed everyone's feet. No one needed his feet washed a second time, did he? But Jesus knew he would be crucified the next day. He knew he was going back to the Father. And he knew his disciples would need to be cleansed again soon. So he commanded his disciples (and today that includes you and me) to wash one another's feet.

How do we wash each other's feet? Naturally, we're not in a position to forgive sins, but God can use us in the process of cleansing. Like Jesus, we can minister to a brother or sister in Christ who has become dirty or defiled by the world.

How often have you asked someone, "How are you?" and he's responded, "Oh, great," but you knew he didn't mean it? Instead of sitting down and gently encouraging that person to open up, we often resort to trivial chatter or simply walk away.

If we're serious about washing one another's feet, we become sensitive to the feelings of others. We pay attention to the verbal and nonverbal signals they give. We discard any judgmental thoughts and ask, "Is something wrong? How are you feeling? Can I pray with you?"

Notice you don't stand up to wash somebody's feet. You

kneel. Humility and servanthood are prerequisites to being used by God.

There's no need to come on strong or pretend we have all the answers. We come on our knees (if not physically, by our attitude) and say, "If I can serve you, if I can be of any help, let me know." By doing that, we can help unleash God's blessing in the lives of others.

One of my team members (I'll call him Greg) was directing a "united" evangelistic crusade in a city where two prominent pastors had fought for years. Many non-Christians knew about the feud between this Presbyterian minister and a Baptist preacher. My associate, Greg, tried to encourage them to patch up their differences, but it was no use.

For the sake of the gospel, Greg decided to call these two pastors together and wash their feet. He invited both pastors to his home for lunch with him and his wife. But he didn't tell either gentleman that the other pastor also was invited. He simply scheduled the Baptist pastor to arrive half an hour earlier than the Presbyterian.

At lunch time the Baptist pastor came over and chatted with Greg while his wife finished preparing lunch. Half an hour later, the Presbyterian minister arrived. Both pastors suddenly stiffened. Greg was scared, but he invited these two men to sit down and quickly got to the point.

"I know you must be shocked—maybe even upset that I've brought you together like this," Greg said. Then he poured out his heart for these two older ministers. "It's my responsibility to bring followers of Jesus together for the upcoming evangelistic crusade. But it isn't happening. And it's because you two men have been fighting. All the Christians know about it. Even many of the non-Christians know you don't love each other, that you've had this bitter resentment against each other. You're hurting the Church and the testimony of the gospel."

"So I feel we shouldn't have lunch today until you ask each other's forgiveness. I'm here to be of any help I can. I realize I'm young, but nobody else in this city would do it. So before the Lord—if you will forgive me—I must be the person to do it."

Both pastors broke down and confessed how they had sinned against each other, harbored resentment in their hearts, and hurt their testimony in that city. Together on their knees they asked for the Lord's forgiveness. And a tremendous break-through occurred.

People quickly learned about the reconciliation of these two pastors. The Baptist pastor, instead of marrying his son and future daughter-in-law in his own church, went over to the Presbyterian church and the two pastors performed the wed-ding ceremony together. As a result, the churches in that city united in an historic way. We had a tremendous evangelistic campaign, with many making first-time decisions for Jesus Christ and several churches planted as a result. It was a thrilling time. But, what would have happened if no one had obeyed the Lord's command? What if no one had humbled himself, and in love washed the feet of those two pastors?

It takes a great measure of love to wash someone's feet. Why else would anyone humbly exhort or rebuke or correct us? Proverbs 9:8 says, "Rebuke a wise man and he will love you." So why don't we wash one another's feet more often? Speaking for myself, I know I can be indifferent toward others. I harbor thoughts like, "I don't want to meddle in that person's life. If I do, he might tell me off. She might hate me. They're going to accuse me of sticking my nose into other people's business."

I believe we cause untold harm whenever we notice someone who is hurting or lacking peace but say nothing. It's obvious our brother or sister has dirty feet. Maybe he's even become defiant in his attitude toward the Lord. Something is wrong, but we ignore it. We don't want to get involved.

A friend of mine was a successful businessman, an elder in his church, and an excellent lay preacher. One day while we were eating out I noticed this friend was eyeing the waitresses. Most men will notice a nice looking woman. But there's a difference between that and looking eagerly with lust in your heart. It seemed to me, and to several others, that our friend was struggling with lust. But because he was a respected Christian leader, we didn't say anything. We were indifferent instead of doing what Scripture says and humbly washing his feet in love.

Looking back, I think our friend would have confessed his sin if we had washed his feet. Instead, one day I received a phone call from a mutual friend. "Luis, I've got bad news. Our friend's wife came over to the house last night, sobbing because she thinks he's having an affair with a secretary at the office."

I couldn't believe the news. Later, while checking in at the airport on my way to Los Angeles, a man accidentally shoved two heavy suitcases against my knee. I turned around and saw it was my friend. He was quite shocked to see me, but pretended nothing was wrong. He quickly said, "Well, Luis! Good to see you. How are you doing?"

Tagging along behind this guy was a young woman...not his wife. At first he tried to distance himself from her, but it was obvious. Besides, his outfit and luggage didn't look right for a business trip. "Uh, Luis, uh, meet Suzie. She's a secretary at my company..."

I wept in my heart because I felt all along that if we had been men of God, four years earlier we could have done something. I should have gone to this friend and said, "Look, we're all tempted, but you don't have to let lust overcome you. Let's look at what God's Word says. Let's get on our knees and take this to the Lord." But I was indifferent, and now it was too late. He was committing adultery.

Later my friend was filled with remorse and regret for what he had done. He repented before the Lord, was reconciled to his wife, and was restored to fellowship in his church. But the scars will always be there—the agony, the suspicion, and all the other pain that follows adultery.

Galatians 6:1 says, "If someone is caught in a sin, you who are spiritual should restore him gently." In Matthew 18:15-17, the Lord gives further instructions if church discipline is in order. And in both of his epistles to the Corinthians, Paul models how to make those instructions work. The goal? To see our fallen brother or sister restored to fellowship with God and with others.

Sin always separates.

If we see someone who seems to be stepping back away from the Lord or a spouse or other believers, there's no time to pretend everything is okay. We need to get on our knees before the Lord and intercede for that person. We need to humble ourselves and admit we're tempted by sin, too. Then we need to go to our friend and gently say, "Listen, can I help you? Is something wrong? I've noticed…"

It's easy to notice when something's wrong in a friend's life and still say nothing. I was speaking at Mount Hermon Conference Center one summer. A seminary professor and his wife on furlough from Asia were there. During the week I chatted briefly with this professor and noticed how sad he looked. I felt the Holy Spirit saying, "Talk to this professor. Find out what's the matter. Try to encourage him."

But I was busy. There were lots of other people to meet. I let it go.

Six months later I found out that while this professor was teaching at the seminary, his wife wrote a little note. He found it on the kitchen table after she had already boarded a plane for the United States. Her note said: "I'm sick and tired of your work at the seminary and all this missionary garbage. Don't come looking for me. I never want to see you again."

That was it. The marriage was over.

Again, I had disobeyed the Holy Spirit. At the time, it seemed ridiculous that a seminary professor needed me to talk to him. But I should have done it anyway. Maybe I could have helped.

I thank the Lord for the men he used early in my ministry to confront me in love about my pride and cockiness and aggressiveness. They were godly men. Men of integrity. They knew what it was to be washed by the Master. And so, even though it was tough, they took me aside and washed my feet.

We all need to be washed. We need the Lord's cleansing. And we need to wash each other's feet. This is a critical step toward radical renewal. But there's more.

After confession and cleansing comes consecration.

ONE THING YOU LACK 5

Several summers ago, two British siblings ran 2,027 miles along the length of the 14 highest mountains in the world. In the process, they climbed a whopping 290,000 feet and traversed 64 mountain passes. The Himalayas furnish some pretty grueling terrain, indeed.

Brothers Richard and Adrian Crane ran their Himalayan trek in a record 101 days, all in hopes of raising money for a British charity. As it turned out, they suffered heat exhaustion, dysentery, heel blisters, torn nails, bruises, and bleeding feet—plus one nasty gash to the head from a rock fall.

In all, the brothers raised $10,700 by journey's end. That works out to less than two cents per thousand steps. One hopes a few more donations have come in since, but I somewhat doubt it.

Imagine trying to accomplish such a mega-marathon feat. Especially if, like the Crane brothers, you had spent only two weekends running through the countryside before flying off to Darjeeling, India, to start your adventure.

The Cranes said their primary training was mental, not physical. You know the concept: "Put your mind to it, and you can do anything." While that doesn't always prove true, we all have a mind for something, whether it's music, money, power, sports, respectability, social status, a happy home, or a comfortable life.

Everybody is dedicated to something. And such is the case for our faith. At some point—either at our conversion or sometime later—we all have to answer some important questions:

- Will I dedicate my life to Jesus?

- Will I make everything else secondary and live for him?

- Will I seek first the kingdom of God and his righteousness?

- Is it true for me that "to live is Christ"?

Jesus' Radical Call

Many Christians think they've dedicated their lives to the Lord, but they haven't given up the rights to certain areas. They haven't dealt with certain sins. They've gone only three-quarters of the way up Calvary's hill, but stopped short of the cross.

Perhaps no other incident in the life and ministry of Jesus emphasizes this issue more than his encounter with a rich young ruler.

From a human point of view, this man had it made. He had his youth. He had inherited immense wealth. He had a prominent social standing. He was religious. He had kept all the commands "since I was a boy," he told Jesus.

But Jesus knew something the young man didn't. He put his finger on the young ruler's wealth. "One thing you lack," Jesus told him. "Go, sell everything you have and give to the poor, and you will have treasure in heaven. Then come, follow me" (Mark 10:21).

The rich young ruler was staggered by Jesus' words. The disciples were staggered, too. And many Christians today still find Jesus' words hard to believe.

"Go, sell, give, come, and follow."

What did he mean?

The rich young man never found out. He walked away, despondent over Jesus' words. What a pity he didn't wait three minutes to hear the Lord say, "I tell you the truth, no one who has left home or brothers or sisters or mother or father or children or fields for me and the gospel will fail to receive *a hundred times as much* in this present age (homes, brothers, sisters, mothers, children and fields—and with them, persecutions) and in the age to come, eternal life" (Mark 10:29-30, emphasis added).

The rich young ruler walked away too quickly. If he had stayed just a few more minutes, he would have realized the Lord was asking for ownership, not demanding possession. I believe the Lord was going to tell him, "Give it to me, but don't worry. You'll get more than enough back." If he had just asked, "Lord, what am I going to do if you take my land? How am I going to live?" The Lord would have said, "Don't worry. I'll give you a hundred times as much. I just want you to understand I have a right to ask for all of it."

Did you catch that?

Jesus has a right to ask for all of it!

What does God want with all of our stuff? He owns the cattle on a thousand hills, so that's not what he is after. He's addressing a bigger issue—the issue of consecration. Are we willing to surrender the rights to everything we own or wish we had? Are we willing to surrender our ambitions and dreams? That's the bottom line of consecration.

As the cross implies, consecration involves immense cost and sacrifice. Jesus said, "If anyone comes to me and does not hate his father and mother, his wife and children, his brothers and sisters—yes, even his own life—he cannot be my disciple. And anyone who does not carry his cross and follow me cannot be my disciple" (Luke 14:25-27).

Those are strong words.

Jesus isn't speaking about a flippant or light-hearted decision. He's talking about radical commitment. No wonder he warned about counting the cost. If you start building a skyscraper but run out of money before it's finished, you end up looking like a fool. Counting the cost is important in the everyday affairs of life; how much more so when it comes to consecration.

When Jesus calls us to consecrate our lives, he's asking for a loyalty and love which dwarfs all else. All other loyalties pale into insignificance and all other loves look like hatred. The Lord is asking for total sacrifice, maximum surrender, the end of "me" and "my rights."

Surrendering Our Rights

A few years back I was speaking at a luncheon in a certain U.S. city. During our gathering, a respected millionaire got up to testify. His main point: "I owe it all to the Lord." During his speech he shared his secret:

"When I was a young fellow, a call was made for me to surrender all. Young as I was, and poor as I was, everything I had I surrendered to Jesus. I didn't have much money, but I put it on the table—all my possessions—and said, 'Jesus, I give everything back to you.' It was after that that God began to bless me. Now I'm a wealthy man."

At that point, a voice from the back of the room shouted, "I challenge you to do it again."

Ever wonder why most of those who respond to the call of a preacher to "surrender all" are young? They don't have that much to surrender—maybe three t-shirts, two pairs of jeans, and their dad's car keys. But when you get to middle age and you own a house and two cars and a condo on the beach—it's a different story.

Surrender is a fundamental aspect of consecration, but today we want little of it. We feel it's our inalienable right to be served. We're told we need to look out for ourselves—give ourselves plenty of "me time."

No doubt we need to look out for ourselves. We need to be sure we take care of our bodies, our spiritual life, etc. But we often take this idea way too far.

A friend of mine once asked me about this area of rights. We were talking about the pressures of traveling on family life, so I explained that I made it a point to spend as much time with the family as possible when home.

But I had to admit I had been less than perfect. In fact, I used to come home and play golf with my pastor, shoot baskets with some friends, or go play tennis with a buddy. Then I realized, this is insane. Here I was, traveling half the time and claiming I couldn't wait to get home to my family. Then when I got home, I went out with my buddies.

Of course, I could argue that I needed the relaxation. I needed time for myself. Time to re-energize or decompress. But that evades the issue. My family comes before all that.

In obedience to Jesus, I gave up the right to spend my free time with friends. It wasn't easy, but it was crucial. Not that I was paying any big price, of course. I don't consider anything we do for Jesus as paying a price. He paid the price, not us. He owns us, not the other way around. But we often rebel against the idea of his Lordship over every area of our life. And many times, we justify it.

There are many hard things the Lord allows in life. Some are his doing. Others are his allowing. Whether it's a move across country, a life without a spouse, a life without children, a crippling disease—all are painful. Some are downright excruciating. But it's not our call.

Offering Our Body as a Living Sacrifice

It's never been easy to surrender our rights, take up our cross, and follow Jesus. As author Chuck Colson wrote once, "The idea of losing our lives for his sake, as Christ tells his disciples to do, is not any more popular today, in our obsessively materialistic society, than it was for the rich young ruler."

By its very nature, biblical consecration is anything but trendy or fashionable. It's much too costly, too life-threatening, too physical. You see this in the life of the apostle Paul. While in a Roman prison, with the threat of execution over his head, Paul could say, "I eagerly expect and hope that I will in no way be ashamed, but will have sufficient courage so that now as always Christ will be exalted in my body, whether by life or by death" (Philippians 1:20).

Paul goes on to say, "For to me, to live is Christ and to die is gain. If I am to go on living in the body, this will mean fruitful labor for me. Yet what shall I choose? I do not know! I am torn between the two: I desire to depart and be with Christ, which is better by far; but it is more necessary for you that I remain in the body" (Philippians 1:21-24).

Did you notice how often Paul talks in this brief passage about his "body"?

As far as Paul knew, his heart was right with God. But he talks here about exalting Jesus "in my body." No doubt he knew he could have his head cut off. He could be fed to the lions. He could be stoned to death at the whim of some corrupt or conniving politician. The Romans had a whole repertoire of miserable ways to die.

But Paul says, "I don't know what to choose—life or death." Which would you choose? Paul honestly struggled whether to accept martyrdom or earnestly pray for release from prison. He had consecrated his body to God.

In 1 Corinthians 6, Paul talks once again about the body. There he explains the utter importance of fleeing from sexual immorality. Why?

Because "All other sins a man commits are outside his body, but he who sins sexually sins against his own body" (6:18). Why is Paul so concerned about the body? What is really at stake?

He gives the answer when he says, "Do you not know that your body is the temple of the Holy Spirit, who is in you, whom you have received from God? You are not your own; you were bought with a price" (6:19-20). That price was the very blood of Jesus, our Savior. "Therefore honor God with your body" (6:20).

Again, Paul has consecration in mind.

That's not all Paul has to say about the body. He talks about it again in Romans 12:1-2, a famous passage that many of us have memorized: "Therefore, I urge you, brothers, in view of God's mercy, to offer your bodies as living sacrifices, holy and pleasing to God—which is your spiritual worship. Do not conform any longer to the pattern of this world, but be transformed by the renewing of your mind. Then you will be able to test and approve what God's will is—his good, pleasing and perfect will."

When Paul says, "I urge you," he isn't making a suggestion or proposal. The Holy Spirit is presenting an urgent message through the mouth of Paul. So what is the message? "Offer your bodies as living sacrifices, holy and pleasing to God— which is your spiritual act of worship." This time our "bodies" are connected with "spiritual worship." Paul says it's a decision every one of us must make.

You can't divorce decisions from the Christian life. Some psychologists say one of the primary causes of emotional breakdowns is irresponsibility—refusing to take responsibility for our actions. Decisions are important! Most people don't like making them, but following Jesus requires certain specific, clearcut decisions.

Have you presented your body as a living sacrifice to the Lord? For many of us, it's the last thing we give up. We give him our spirit and say, "Lord, save me." We give him our soul and say, "Lord, keep me happy and balanced." But the body? It's the last citadel we allow God to capture. Yet the Lord Jesus said, "Whoever wants to save his life will lose it, but whoever loses his life for me and for the gospel will save it" (Mark 8:35).

So why do we try to cling to our body so desperately? In my case, I think it was a combination of ignorance, spiritual blindness, ingrained self-centeredness, and basic distrust of the goodness of God.

Really, all of those reasons revolved around my stubborn refusal to honor the Lord and consecrate myself to him. As I explained in Chapter 1, that's when my first big spiritual crisis (after salvation) began.

I believe God brings every believer to this point of crisis. If we refuse, he brings us back to this crisis point again and again. Many of us live in that cycle for years. And sadly, if we're insistent on going our own way, there comes a time when the Lord says, "I will only push you so far."

Not Holding Back

Consecration is an act of the will. It's a personal crisis before the Lord with immense consequences. We can't hold back in any area. The Lord wants all or nothing. And he deserves a clear, straightforward answer.

Until we give him our body, we've given him nothing at all.

With consecration comes conflict. Remember, we're in a spiritual battle. Consecration is a direct threat to the world's dominion in our lives. The world won't go down without a fight. The moment we say, "Lord Jesus, you asked for my body and here it is," we're automatically saying no to worldly talk, worldly thought, worldly things.

The decision to consecrate ourselves to God is tough, especially for those who find themselves enchanted by the world. The funny thing is, the world doesn't care a thing about you and me.

When I was young I tried to please the world. I tried desperately to win the flattery of those around me. Thankfully, the

Lord dealt with me and brought me to a point of crisis. I felt like God was saying, "Luis, just a few more days of living like this and you're finished." I could see it coming. I'd been walking away from God for several years. I'd pushed things to the limit. That's when I got down on my knees and said, "Lord, have mercy. I'll serve you and give my whole life to you." Having made that simple yet profound decision, my life began to change radically.

If you're tired of catering to the world's latest fads, if you're weary of giving in to the lusts of the flesh, if you've had it trying to live like the devil, you must take this next step. Don't play games with God. Don't miss out on everything God still has in store for you. Dedicate your life to him today. Don't let another hour go by.

Perhaps you made this decision years ago as a young man or young woman. You may have even gone forward at a special camp or church meeting. You began to enjoy the Christian life in a new way. But then later something happened. You gave in to sexual temptation. You married a non-Christian. You cheated in college or in a business deal. You've never forgotten the matter, and you shouldn't forget it until you ask for forgiveness.

The fact is, you used to be happy in the Lord. But since that setback, a huge spiritual parenthesis has loomed in your life. You've had no victory. No joy. No growth. If that's the case, why not consecrate your life anew? Say, "Lord, I put myself back on your altar again. I'm all yours. Take my body. Fill my heart. I give myself to you."

I make no apology about repeatedly urging you to consecrate your life to God, because the day I made this decision was a day of new beginnings for me. Is God speaking to you? My prayer is that the truths of God's Word, especially Romans 12:1-2, will move you to make this step. Offer your body as a living sacrifice, holy and pleasing to God. It's an act of worship. It's a rational decision of the will.

Consecration Involves Both a Crisis and a Process

This crisis of consecration leads to a process that continues for the rest of our lives. Consecration isn't a one-time decision we never think about again. It doesn't permanently eliminate conflict in our souls.

The process of consecration involves continuous, ongoing obedience and submission to God. It means repeatedly surrendering our natural rights for the greater spiritual good. Jesus had a right not to die. He had a right not to be spat upon, cruelly mocked, and beaten unmercifully. Yet he didn't make use of those rights. He allowed himself to be scourged and crucified for the greater good, in obedience to the Father's will.

Likewise, every time our will crosses God's revealed will, we have to make a decision. If we choose his revealed will over and against our own, then we're surrendering our rights. We're consecrating our lives. If we don't choose his will, we're doomed.

This is what Scripture means when it speaks of the death of Jesus, of taking up the cross, of the grain of wheat falling into the ground and dying. Whenever I choose God's revealed will, it is death to my ego. Death to my pride. Death to my ambitions and dreams.

Every decision in life is another opportunity to say yes to God, to affirm his Lordship over our body, soul, and spirit. Each time I choose God's will over my own, I'm becoming more and more like Jesus. I'm testing and approving his will, that which is good and acceptable and perfect.

This is what it means to live in triumph and victory. Suddenly, we're no longer faced with decisions like whether to marry a non-Christian, whether to cheat on an expense account, whether to give in to temptation. What could be a terrible struggle gives way to tremendous relief. The issue is settled. By gladly choosing God's will, we're free to move ahead with renewed strength and vigor. We're no longer playing games with God. We still face our enemies—the world, the flesh, and the devil—but now we enjoy victory and walk in holy boldness as ambassadors for Christ.

Consecrating Your Life Today

It's not too late to return to the living God and consecrate yourself to him. Will you take that step? Perhaps you'd like to join me in this prayer of dedication:

"Oh God, solemnly in your presence I present my body as a living sacrifice, holy and pleasing to you. Here is my body, as a symbol of all that I am. It's yours. I can't wait to see what you're going to do in and through my life for the glory of your name, Amen."

This could be the most exciting experience of your life. You can now walk by faith, in great expectation, wondering what God is going to do. You will have your ups and downs. You will have your moments of darkness. But when you make this commitment, it's amazing what can begin to happen.

And now that we've dealt with the cross, it's time to personally experience the resurrection!

Are you ready?

CHRIST IN YOU 6

When I think of the power of God at work in someone's life, I often think of Gladys Aylward. She has rightly been called the most noted single woman missionary of the twentieth century. If you'd met Gladys in her younger days, however, you would have wondered what all the fuss was about. Born into a working-class family, Gladys did poorly in school and began working as a maid at the age of 14. She would have remained a maid for life if God had not intervened.

A pastor's wife with a passion for the lost won Gladys to the Lord. After her conversion in her mid-twenties, Gladys began dreaming of telling the lost about her Savior. And not just in her corner of London where she worked. She felt distinctly called by God to go to China.

The mission board to which she applied couldn't have been less enthusiastic. That didn't hinder Gladys. She set out by train across Europe and Asia. That she made it to China is a miracle.

Once in China, God allowed Gladys to undergo some harrowing experiences, but used her to win many Chinese to himself. She demonstrated courage and physical endurance where many a man would have wilted. The secret wasn't her background, education, or missionary training. By all those standards, she didn't measure up. But because her life was centered on God alone, he was pleased to demonstrate his power through her.

God wants to show his power in and through each of us, whatever our circumstances and calling in life. And although consecration is essential, by itself it isn't enough.

Zeal for God Isn't Enough

The greatest fact in all of history is that the Lord has chosen to come and indwell us. Think of it. Almighty God lives in us. This fact revolutionized my life when I understood it for the first time. I already had dedicated and rededicated my life to Jesus probably a dozen times. Every time, I took off with great zeal and high expectations only to come crashing back down to reality.

The problem was I was zealously trying to sweat it out for God. Always trying to be faithful. Always trying to overcome temptation by sheer dedication, discipline, Bible study, and prayer. It was Luis and his friends trying and trying and trying to be faithful to the Lord.

We were honest. We were sincere. We were zealous. We tried just about everything to win people to Jesus. Some would listen. Others would ridicule. But we saw few trust Jesus as Savior. My life felt fruitless and futile and frustrated.

Up to that time, I had been self-confident and ego-centered. "God, you really got yourself a prize in me. I tell you, Lord, I'm going to be dedicated 'til death. If I have to die for the kingdom, I'll die." In my little heart was a feeling that "I'm going to show the world what a young man can do for God."

It was a sincere desire, but it was absurd.

I quickly learned that trying to live for God in your own strength gets you nothing but exhausted. Even a zealous, dedicated, consecrated Christian cannot live for God. We can clench our teeth, tighten our fists, and grimly determine we're going to pray, read the Bible, study, witness, and live for God alone. But after a while even the most zealous Christian will end up feeling discouraged.

God can hardly wait for us to admit we can't live the Christian life as he intended. Why? Because the only person who could ever live the Christian life was Jesus Christ himself. Frankly, it's only when we're defeated, when we're flat on our faces, when we're completely wiped out, that we're ready to discover the greatest truth of the Christian life.

It's futile trying to please God in our own strength. But, praise the Lord, he is pleased to live in us. This is the fact that changed my life:

Each one of us is united with Jesus, and he wants to manifest his resurrection life through us—if only we let him.

The apostle Paul said, "I want to know Christ and the power of his resurrection and the fellowship of sharing in his sufferings, becoming like him in his death" (Philippians 3:10). We have to be crucified with Christ, however, before the power of his resurrection life can surge through us.

This is more than a consecrated life for Christ.

Most of us are so stubborn that it takes years before we learn to truly die to self. We resist it with all our might. We fight and rebel against it. We hold on to our lives, try to honor him in our own strength. And inevitably, we find ourselves frustrated. "What are you doing?" we cry out to God. "Are you trying to tell me I don't have what it takes?"

That's exactly what God is trying to tell us. We don't have what it takes to live for his glory. But he does. And all his resources are ours!

Do you believe that?

The Heart of the New Testament

Even though most of us didn't understand it at the time, becoming a Christian is tantamount to being invaded. "He who unites himself with the Lord is one with him in spirit" (1 Corinthians 6:17).

It's no longer God up there, and you and me down here. We're no longer separated. We don't talk to God at a distance. We're one spirit now.

God has taken up residence within us!

In Revelation, Jesus says, "Here I am! I stand at the door and knock. If anyone hears my voice and opens the door, I will come in and eat with him, and he with me" (3:20). Although this works wonderfully as an illustration for someone to trust Jesus Christ, it's really a word to us as Christians.

Jesus is speaking about our heart. He says it has a door that can be opened only from the inside. He will never try to smash it open. He simply knocks. Only we can open the door and let him in. The question is: Will we?

"How do I open the door?" you ask. It's as if I were to go to your house tonight and knock on your front door. You look out the window and say, "Oh my goodness. It's Luis Palau!" You have to make a decision. You can either let me in, or keep me out. It's up to you.

If you decide to let me in, all you have to do is open the door and say, "Come in, Luis. Sit down. Take off your coat. What would you like to drink?"

That's what Jesus is saying to us. "I stand at your door. I am knocking. Have you heard my call?" he says. "Please, open the door and I will come in and eat with you and you with me." In other words, we will experience the fullness of his presence in our lives. And what a delight that is.

Do you believe that God lives in you?

Are you enjoying that reality?

I'd like to challenge you to discover this truth in the scriptures for yourself. Try underlining every verse you can find that speaks of God indwelling us. You'll be amazed at all the references—especially in the Gospel of John and the epistles. This is what I consider the heart of the New Testament message.

Let me give you a sampling. In Matthew 1:23, Jesus is named "Immanuel"— "God with us." That's only the start. God is now in us and wants to fill us completely.

Paul asks, "Do you not know that your body is a temple of the Holy Spirit, who is in you, whom you have received from God?" (1 Corinthians 6:19). Whether your body is fat or skinny, tall or short—if you're a Christian, God dwells in you.

That's why the thought of sexual immorality should be so repulsive to a Christian. When we trusted Jesus, our body became a sanctuary for God's Holy Spirit. Anything that would grieve him should grieve us. To think that we would defile God's temple is horrifying. God no longer says, "Take off your sandals—this is holy ground." He says, "Put off your old ways— you now are to be holy, just as I who indwell you am holy."

To perceive this marvelous truth is to wonder, "Oh Lord, why did it take me so long to understand that the secret of the Christian life, the central theme of the New Testament, is Christ living in me?"

People will object. They think the foundation of the message of the New Testament is the work of Jesus on the cross. It is. But why did Jesus go to the cross? Because he wants to fill us. And he couldn't indwell us until we had been cleansed of sin. And that couldn't happen until his work was done on the cross.

The cross was a necessary preliminary step for God's ultimate objective, which is to unite us with himself forever.

Galatians 2:20 ties these two issues together. It says, "I have been crucified with Christ and I no longer live, but Christ lives in me. The life I live in the body, I live by faith in the Son of God, who loved me and gave himself for me."

Notice the twin truths of this verse. First, "I have been crucified with Christ." From God's perspective, we are dead to sin. Sin has nothing to do with us and we have nothing to do with it. From our perspective, we hate sin. We hate it in ourselves; we hate it in other people. We never want to touch it again. When we fall into it, we quickly confess our sins and step back into God's light. This is the attitude of crucifixion.

The second truth is, "Christ lives in me." This is the key to leaving the desert and embracing radically renewed faith. Other facts and practices must go along, yet we experience God's renewal within us only when you and I understand and accept this truth—Jesus literally lives in us!

It's not enough to be consecrated. There's a danger in looking back at the day when we took Romans 12:1-2 to heart and dedicated our lives to Jesus Christ. Yes, we need to know that at some point we put ourselves on the altar, so to speak. But, victory doesn't come from looking back and rejoicing over that decision.

The Lord desires that we enjoy the fact that Jesus lives in us. The resurrected life of Jesus in me is a living truth, not an experience we had sometime in the past.

For some reason, most Christians have not taken this important step in their walk with Christ. That's why you meet so many people who are consecrated but powerless. They've definitely made a commitment to Jesus. They can show you the date of their commitment written on the front leaf of their Bible. But they're powerless. They're depressed and can't seem to rise above their circumstances.

In Philippians 4:12, Paul talks about his circumstances: "I know what it is to be in need, and I know what it is to have plenty. I have learned the secret of being content in any and every situation, whether well fed or hungry, whether living in plenty or in want."

Adverse circumstances didn't leave him down.

The question is how Paul learned that. Where did he get that kind of adaptability? Most of us don't handle poverty very well, or riches for that matter. How did Paul do it? His secret: "I can do everything through him who gives me strength" (4:13). Jesus Christ was Paul's source of strength in every situation.

In Colossians 1:27, Paul speaks of "the glorious riches of this mystery, which is Christ in you, the hope of glory." This truth so thrilled Paul that he labored—"struggling with all his energy, which so powerfully works in me"—to proclaim it throughout the Roman Empire. Paul wasn't striving in his own energy. The key to his amazing influence was "Christ living and working in me."

Paul talks about this again in Colossians 2:9-10. In Christ "the whole fullness of deity dwells bodily, and you have come to fullness of life in him, who is the head of all rule and authority" (RSV).

If Jesus Christ is God, and he is, and if he indwells every believer, and he does, then all the fullness of God indwells us. Not because we're something, but because the One who is everything fills us!

Was this theme merely a favorite subject of Paul's, or the very heartbeat of our Savior?

Consider the Lord's High Priestly prayer in John 17. Fervently he prayed that all believers "may be one, Father, just as you are in me and I am in you. May they also be in us so that the world may believe that you have sent me. I have given them the glory that you gave me, that they may be one as we are one: I in them and you in me. May they be brought to complete unity to let the world know that you sent me and have loved them even as you have loved me" (17:21-23). What an amazing prayer he prayed for you and me!

What temptation could you face that Jesus does not have the power to overcome? What need might I have that the living Lord Jesus cannot meet? What wisdom will we ever need that he cannot provide?

If this truth grips your heart, it will revolutionize your life. Yet most of the Christians I meet know nothing of the fullness of God. They have never experienced the joy and power and victory of the Christ-centered life. They haven't recognized that it's not enough to receive Jesus Christ (John 1:12), to open the door of their heart to him (Revelation 3:20).

The Lord doesn't want to simply take up residence in our lives. Sure, he indwells every believer. But, he wants to fill every fiber of our being! Do you remember what he said?

"I am the vine; you are the branches. If a man remains in me and I in him, he will bear much fruit; apart from me you can do nothing" (John 15:5).

Have you ever looked at a grapevine? It's often almost impossible to tell where the vine stops and the branches begin. They're intricately connected to one another. They "abide" in each other. Working together, they produce much fruit.

Scripture isn't speaking symbolically or figuratively about Jesus' desire to "abide" in us. As branches, we are entirely connected with the true Vine. We're one spirit. Nothing can separate us. He indwells us. We can do all things through Christ, who wants us to bear much fruit for his Father's glory. He wants to control and bless everything we think and do and say. Abiding in him is a fact we need to understand and act upon day by day. It isn't a decision we make: "I must abide with Christ. I must become a fruitful branch." Jesus said we're already branches. We're joined to him, and without him, we can do nothing.

The problem is many Christians don't understand the Christ-centered life. When they understand it, they find it hard to believe. And when they believe it, they find it hard to know how to take hold of what Jesus has to offer and live it out day after day. If they did, the Church would be a powerhouse!

Can you imagine millions of Christians who actually believed—as they drive to work and go about their tasks—that God indwells them? Christians who lived in "conscious, constant communion" with Jesus Christ? The power would be incredible. Even with the weaknesses we all have, the power would be tremendous.

It can happen. All the resources of Jesus are entirely at our disposal. Because he indwells us, all that belongs to Jesus belongs to us. Yet how little we draw from those infinite resources.

The Day Christ Took Over

No one can live the Christian life except Jesus Christ himself. I'll never forget the look on the face of an older missionary in Colombia, sometime later, when this truth dawned on him. I'd been asked to speak to a group of missionaries at a conference during my first year on the field. My theme was the indwelling Christ as our resource and power to serve.

Afterward, this old missionary gentleman invited me to go for a walk with him. With tears streaming down his face, he told me, "Luis, I have been here on the field for more than 30 years. Everybody thinks I'm a great pioneer missionary. Yes, I've planted a few churches because I've preached the gospel. But my wife and I have never had joy. We've talked about it for hours. Why don't we enjoy the Christian life? Why is it such a chore? Why do we always seem to be struggling?

"I've worked for God as hard as I could, with every ounce of my being, but it's brought little but frustration. Now I see why. Until today, I don't think I have ever really known what it means to allow the risen Jesus to do the living in me. Why didn't someone tell me about this before?"

My heart went out to this old man, a genuine servant of the Lord, but one who had so little joy in his life. This fantastic truth doesn't sink in easily.

This reality is for you. You must make a decision. Are you going to let Jesus control you from within? The Bible teaches that if you want a fruitful life, if you want victory to overcome tempta-tion, if you want power and authority, then it can't be you. It must be Jesus.

This decision revolutionized my life. When I finally made the decision to hand my life fully over to the Lord, at last I experi-enced power, authority, victory, freedom, and joy. I finally un-derstood what Paul meant when he said, "If anyone is in Christ, he is a new creation; the old has gone, the new has come!" (2 Corinthians 5:17). The Lord changed the way I thought, the way I felt about people, the whole way I went about life.

Too many Christians live the way I lived for too many years. They believe that if they pray enough, read enough, and work enough, they'll be victorious. That's the work of the flesh, the essence of self. It cannot be done. We cannot work or earn our victories through self-effort, any more than we could work for our salvation.

Fullness vs. Fruitless Frustration

I've been in Christian service more than 50 years, long enough to tell you by name the stories of dozens of people who had great potential for God. I've known men who were tremendous expositors, preachers, teachers, and musicians who spiritually are on the bench today. Some committed gross sins. Others just ran out of energy because they were using the gifts of God with the fire of the flesh.

Unless you and I are living in the power of God, we're going to run out of gas. We're going to be cruising along and suddenly lose power. We'll be idled and sidelined, or worse, because we were operating in the flesh.

Many of us were brought up with the concept, "Now that you're saved, roll up your sleeves. Work for Christ, fight the devil, overcome sin, live for God, grit your teeth, get out there and be a good witness."

We should be active and fruitful, but in dependence upon a source other than ourselves. It doesn't come automatically. But as we consciously depend on God as our ultimate source of power and strength, we're renewed and revitalized. We never have to worry about an energy shortage because God's resources are unlimited.

Look at the example of Robert Murray McCheyne, a famous Scottish preacher and man of God during the 19th century. He died when he was only 29 years old. But even as a young man, McCheyne was a spiritual giant. They say that when he would get up to the pulpit, people would start crying before he said a single word. Now that's the power of God in someone's life!

On one occasion McCheyne told a friend in a letter, "According to your holiness, so shall be your success.... Mr. Edwards, a holy man is an awesome weapon in the hand of God."

Are we an awesome weapon in the hands of God? We can be, if his power is at work through us.

Starting Each Day Renewed

Nothing is more important than starting the day off right. I begin each day with a prayer of thanks to God—as soon as my eyes open and my feet hit the floor. It sounds cliché, but it makes all the difference.

Beginning your day with a prayer of thanksgiving to God isn't as easy as it sounds. It takes practice and determination.

For years I groaned about each new day. My prayers—when I prayed—were more complaints than praise. "Lord, here comes another day. I don't feel up to the tasks before me. There are so many temptations. I don't want to lose my temper. Don't let me fail you. Don't let me grieve you. Don't let me dishonor you if an opportunity to witness comes up." On and on I went, groaning and moaning, wailing and pleading with the Lord.

I remember frequently praying, "Don't leave me, Lord," as if Hebrews 13:5-6 could be turned around to say, "I am going to leave you and forsake you. Don't count on me. Watch out for what others are going to do to you!" God must have thought my prayers were utter foolishness.

Then one day Fred Renich, who helped direct our missionary internship program, challenged me and several others in this area. He claimed that "most of you probably start out the day groaning. The content, tone, and direction of your prayers are negative." And he was right.

I hadn't realized how negative I was.

Renich made it clear he wasn't advocating positive thinking as a cure-all. He taught us how prayers of thanksgiving are different. How they are based on the promises and reality of God. He urged us to start each day saying prayers like, "Thank you, Lord Jesus. Here's a new day. Yes, I'm weak, but you are strong and all your resources are my resources. I don't always know how to witness to others, but you'll give me the right words. When temptation comes, Lord, I've got your power. Thank you that you have all power in heaven and on earth. Thank you that you live in me. Thank you that your resurrection life is real and that today you're going to prove it once again."

Why start the day with a prayer of unbelief? Why not start with a note of praise?

If I understand Romans 4:20 correctly, Abraham grew strong in his faith as he gave glory to God. God had promised the impossible—his wife, almost 90 years old, would have a son. The temptation to doubt God was incredible. But Abraham became "fully persuaded that God had power to do what he had promised" (4:21).

Are you convinced that same power of God is in you? Affirm it at the beginning of each day.

Staying Renewed Throughout the Day

You may be thinking, "But, Luis, what about the rest of the day? It's one thing to start the day off right. But what about when I face temptation?"

The living Lord Jesus has all the power we'll ever need. The fact that we're cleansed and consecrated and Christ-centered doesn't mean trials and temptations will bypass us.

Temptations are a fact of life. Temptations to cheat, to lie, to be shady in business dealings. Temptations to do what might be embarrassing or even shameful. You can get up in the morning, have your devotions, sing a chorus of praise to the Lord, pray, kiss your spouse goodbye, and review a memory verse on the way to work, only to see something you didn't intend to see, or think something you didn't intend to think. Temptation suddenly jumps out at you. What do you do?

Honesty is always the best policy.

The Lord indwells us and knows every thought. You can say, "Lord Jesus, thank you that you indwell me. You see what I see. You know how I feel. You know what temptation just hit me. Thank you for your power at work in me. Thank you for keeping me pure and holy, so that I can give glory to your name."

In one of his beautiful hymns, Charles Wesley wrote that Jesus "breaks the power of canceled sin, he sets the prisoner free."

Temptation loses its grip. "Sin will have no dominion over you" (Romans 6:14 RSV). Why? Because we're not under the law, trying our best to live for God. Instead, in his grace, "Christ lives in me."

True Christianity is life. It's "the life of God in the soul of man" (Henry Scougal). That's the whole reason Jesus came. And he desires that we enjoy this life to the full. If he is in your heart, his power is in you. It's the same power that raised Jesus from the dead. And now it can resurrect you—today!

When God's resurrection power is at work within us on a daily basis, there's no reason to sweat and try to do the best we can in our own strength.

Yes, we are called to work hard.

Yes, we should sweat and work and toil and plod along. But it isn't what we do for Jesus, but what he does through us.

Yes, we work—but not relying on our own power.

Yes, we want to walk in the light—but we can't be holy unless he makes us holy.

Therefore, we rely on his presence to make us holy and transparent. We couldn't do it on our own, any more than Moses or Paul. God is there to make it happen.

And that changes everything.

Balanced Every Step of the Way

I often think that a man or woman walking in the power of the indwelling Christ is like a tightrope walker.

I still remember the high-wire act that came to my town in Argentina when I was a boy. Some German performers came and stretched an enormous cable between two buildings over the plaza of the city where I lived. The cable must have been 100 feet off the ground, but the performers didn't set up any safety nets. Starting from opposite ends, they walked across the high wire and played games with the crowd.

The street was filled with a huge crowd below. Everyone thought they were going to fall to their deaths as they swayed back and forth, used long poles to keep their balance, then traded poles as they tried to get past each other. In fact, one of the performers did slip but caught the cable and pulled himself back up. In the end, they made it across the high wire just fine.

Living under the control of Jesus is just like that. There's a tremendous amount of excitement. People may look at you and say, "He's not going to make it," but you keep your balance as you walk with the indwelling Christ. He's the pole that keeps you in balance every step of the way.

God's ultimate objective is to take complete control and mold his character in us. It's not me trying to be holy, trying to be perfect, trying to conform to the image of God. It's Jesus indwelling and filling me that makes the difference.

I'm not passive. I'm acting in his power. Any power I have is really his in me. Jesus has become my wisdom, my righteousness and sanctification and redemption" (1 Corinthians 1:30 RSV). That's why Paul says, "Let him who boasts, boast in the Lord" (1 Corinthians 1:31).

No wonder Jesus says, "Let your light shine before men, that they may see your good works and praise your Father in heaven" (Matthew 5:16). The good that people see in you and me is Jesus shining through. He is our light, our source of true life. The more we look to him, the more we reflect his glory—being transformed into his likeness with ever-increasing glory, which comes from him (2 Corinthians 3:18).

God is relentlessly at work to transform us. He has no intention of waiting to start the job in the life to come. God already has begun his good work in us, and he "will carry it on to completion until the day of Christ" (Philippians 1:6). He intends to make us "conformed to the likeness of his son" (Romans 8:29).

So why don't we let him?

Just think of it for a moment. God is at work within us—filling us with himself. What possibilities come with that reality! I can't imagine anything else that will truly transform a person.

God himself dwells within me! That alone is a motivation for holy, bold living. That alone compels us to ask, "Lord, what is on your heart? How do you want me to feel, act, and think? What do you want to do through me here on earth for your glory?"

This heart-felt prayer leads to the discovery of God's passion, which is to fill us with his compassion for a lost and hurting world. Out of radical renewal comes a desire to take the love of Jesus to those who know nothing of it.

Do you have that passion? Do you want to see God use you to introduce others to his son? Then hang on! The Christ-controlled life naturally leads to heart-felt evangelism.

PASSION FOR THE LOST

7

During preparation for one of our evangelistic crusades in Latin America some years ago, a very poor, shoeless, unshaven man attended one of our week-long biblical counseling courses.

Generally, the better educated, socially established, and spiritually mature lay leaders of the local churches attend this in-depth training course. Not by design, of course. That just seems to be what happens. So it was unusual to see such a poor man participating, especially considering he was illiterate. Although he attended every class, we didn't expect him to do much counseling. Little did we realize how much he really learned.

Several weeks later, during our campaign, we were inundated with people seeking counsel. One evening, every available counselor was busy—all except for the illiterate man.

That's when a doctor walked in—refined, sophisticated, well-dressed. He was clearly upper-class, and he was requesting counsel.

Before anyone could stop him, the shabbily dressed man took the doctor into a room to talk. When our director discovered what happened, he was a bit concerned. When the doctor came out of the room, the director asked if he could help him in any way. "No, thank you." The doctor replied, "This fellow has helped me very much!"

The next day the doctor returned with two other doctors. Our director wanted to talk with them personally, but the doctor refused. They wanted the shoeless, illiterate man.

By the end of the week, that illiterate man had led four doctors and their wives to Jesus Christ. What a servant! He couldn't read or write, but he lived a victorious Christian life.

So often we look on the outside when measuring someone else's spirituality. What really counts is the power of Jesus within. That's the secret to radical renewal, as we saw in the last chapter. Overflowing from such renewal comes a deep, growing, heartfelt passion for the things of God.

When we're filled with God, our hearts are burdened by the same things that burden him. So what's on God's heart? First and foremost, He's concerned about reconciling people to himself. The Lord isn't willing that any perish, but wants everyone to come to repentance (2 Peter 3:9).

How can we get that same overriding passion for lost souls?

Genuine concern for the lost doesn't come naturally. By nature we're selfish. As long as we have our own little goodies, we're happy. But when you're filled with God, it isn't long before you say, "God, give me a passion to see people come to know you. You've done so much for me. I want everyone to experience your salvation. I want to see you at work in others."

A passion for the lost isn't something we're taught. I'm all for motivating and training Christians for sharing the truth. In fact, part of my evangelistic association's vision is "to stimulate, revive and mobilize the Church to continuous, effective evangelism, follow-up, and church growth." Thousands of people take our friendship evangelism training course before our festivals. And a good number of them have the opportunity to lead someone to Jesus. But training itself can't stir a concern for the destiny of lost souls.

When the Holy Spirit is overflowing in our lives, we automatically begin to share the gospel with others. Jesus told his disciples, "You will receive power when the Holy Spirit comes on you; and you will be my witnesses . . ." (Acts 1:8). And that's exactly what happened. Formerly timid Galileans became holy, bold witnesses for his name.

The same can be true of us today. In fact, the same should be true.

Take my father-in-law, a wonderful man who went to be with the Lord several years ago. He was such a quiet guy. I couldn't imagine him saying more than a couple of lines trying to witness to others. But he had a deep burden for his old college buddies. As a result, anytime I spoke in town, he brought one or more of them. He could never be a public speaker, and he didn't want to be. But that's not what a passion for the lost is all about.

Some people complain they don't have the gift of evangelism.

They think they never could preach the gospel like me. And the fact is, they are probably right. But they don't have to!

You can have the same deep heart of compassion for the lost even if you don't have the gift of evangelism.

The secret isn't striving to get some gift God never intended to give you. The secret is living and witnessing by the power of the indwelling Lord. That's true whether you're a Sunday school teacher who takes a special concern for that one lost kid in your class, or a talented musician who uses his musical gift to the glory of God.

The Bible says, "He who is faithful in a very little thing is faithful also in much" (Luke 16:10 NASB). Be faithful where you are, and the Lord will begin to open doors for you. When you witness as an overflow from a heart filled by God's Spirit, people will sense your love and concern. And trust me, amazing things will happen as a result.

The Day of the Laid-Back Evangelical

Tragically, a gripping passion for the lost is a rare commodity today. This is the day of the laid-back evangelical.

I heard a speaker at my church say, "When I was younger, I worked with Campus Crusade. I used to buttonhole everybody. I used to witness to anything that moved. And even some things that didn't move."

The speaker was trying to be funny, implying that he'd "matured" beyond that point. But I've been in this country now for many years and I've never been buttonholed by a Christian. I wish somebody would try to witness to me.

Billy Graham once told me that in the days of the Jesus People movement, he had walked down the Sunset Strip in Hollywood one day and in one three-block stretch was buttonholed three times. It made him weep.

It would make me weep.

I wish people were actively witnessing for Jesus. Why do Christians sometimes make fun of such things? Because people love to hear sarcasm. They want to be laid back. No one wants to come across as impatient or overbearing or pushy. But how can we have that attitude when people all around us are going to hell?

The closest anyone has come to buttonholing me was in London. I was walking down a street with one of our British board members when we came to a street fair. Thousands of people were crowded together. No sooner had I said, "Someone should be passing out invitations to our campaign," than this young man seemingly jumps out and gives me an invitation. I said, "Hello, brother, thanks for doing this. I'm Luis Palau." (He was shocked to say the least. He had just invited me to my own campaign.) Other than that, no one has tried to witness to me in more than 50 years.

Why do the majority of Christians lack any concern for the unsaved? Because they've never experienced God's radical renewal in their own life.

"Come, follow me." Jesus said, "and I will make you fishers of men" (Matthew 4:19). It's only as we wholeheartedly follow Jesus that we gain his passion for the lost.

Cultivating a Heart of Compassion

As we follow Jesus, what can we do to cultivate his heart of compassion for those who are "harassed and helpless, like sheep without a shepherd" (Matthew 9:36)?

First, we can pray.

"The harvest is plentiful but the workers are few. Ask the Lord of the harvest, therefore, to send out workers into his harvest field" (Matthew 9:37-38). We can pray for workers, both for those already actively involved in evangelism and cross-cultural missions, and for those yet to be sent out.

We can also pray for those who have yet to trust Jesus. Make a list of the unsaved family members, friends, neighbors, and others you know from school or work who need Jesus. Get on your knees and pray regularly for each person by name. Be persistent in your prayers. Think long-term.

To God, no amount of time is too long to pray for someone.

My wife and I know an elderly woman who prayed for 68 years for her brother's salvation. When he was 80 years old, shortly before he died, he confessed the Lord Jesus as Savior. Some may think, "That was by the skin of his teeth!" but the benefit was not only his. Imagine the tremendous blessing in that woman's life resulting from 68 years of faithful prayer.

Of course, sometimes God answers our prayers quickly. A friend took up my challenge to pray by name for the salvation of five businessmen he knows. Then we got together for lunch a few weeks later. The Lord already had given him the opportunity to witness to one of those five business friends, who surrendered his life to Jesus. You can imagine how excited my friend was. And you better believe he wanted to keep praying for the other four.

A teenage girl I met in Scotland took up a similar challenge, praying by name for ten of her friends at school. Within a year all ten had trusted Jesus as Savior. This girl was elated. Many others have told me similar stories.

Second, study what the Bible says about eternity.

Read all the passages in the New Testament that talk about the eternal condemnation of the lost. You'll discover Scripture teaches those who reject Jesus to their dying day go to hell— "the lake of fire."

Note what Jesus himself says in the Gospels: "Do not be afraid of those who kill the body but cannot kill the soul. Rather, be afraid of the One [God] who can destroy both soul and body in hell" (Matthew 10:28).

On many occasions Jesus warned about being "in danger of the fire of hell" or being "thrown into hell." Concerning his Church, Jesus said, "The gates of Hades will not overcome it" (Matthew 16:18).

Third, believe absolutely what the Bible says about the eternal condition of the lost.

Let the Lord's words about the hopelessness and agony of the lost sink in. He speaks of hell as a place of weeping, wailing, and gnashing of teeth.

Some try to explain away what the Bible teaches about hell. Or they ask, "If people die rejecting Jesus Christ, are they really going to be lost forever?"

The simple, biblical answer – "Yes!"

It takes a while for that to really sink in. Most of us would like to believe that somehow, at the end of history, after people have been in hell for a thousand years, the Lord will say, "Let's have a general amnesty. Let's bring the poor souls up to paradise." In fact, some very popular authors have written on the subject recently. It has become a very, very popular view.

There is just one problem—it's not true.

That's not what the Bible teaches. Of course, it's what so many—even in evangelical circles—would like to believe. And frankly, I believe it's why many Christians don't have a passion for souls. We refuse to believe that if someone rejects Jesus up to his dying day, he's really lost forever and there's no hope.

If we believed the Bible absolutely, our thinking would change dramatically. Instead of halfheartedly wishing an unsaved friend or relative would be saved, we would realize, "If he has an accident and dies tomorrow, he's going to hell forever." When that hits home, it drives us to want to win that person to Jesus.

If we believe what the Bible says about the lost, we're going to want to spend time alone with God. We're going to pray for God to give us a passion for those who don't yet know him. We're going to desperately ask the Lord to give us a value for souls that is beyond ourselves.

I prayed that prayer 50 years ago and haven't felt laid back since. How can I stay home, comfortable and content? I know where people go when they die if they don't know Jesus. How can I do nothing?

Developing a Lifestyle of Soul-winning

The Bible says, "The fruit of the righteous is a tree of life, and he who wins souls is wise" (Proverbs 11:30). I know this verse is batted around as if it had nothing to do with a passion for the lost. But let's carefully look at what it says.

First, if we are righteous, if we are walking with God in the light of his presence, then we're a tree of life. And what greater fruit could anyone bear than bringing the message of eternal life to those he or she loves?

Some of your friends and relatives who don't know the Lord may seem hardened against the gospel. From your perspective, it may appear there is no hope for their conversion. But don't become unconcerned or apathetic. Continue to live righteously because "the fruit of the righteous is a tree of life." It brings forth fruit in its season.

Second, God says, "And he (or she) who wins souls is wise" (Proverbs 11:30). I've heard people say that phrase is outdated, but it's still in the Bible and I happen to like it.

Scripture says God created man, breathed into him, and he became "a living soul" (Genesis 2:7 KJV). You and I are living souls. Someday our bodies will fall apart. No amount of medicine or vitamins or exercise can prevent that from happening. But our soul lives forever. It will never die. That's why the Bible says he or she who wins souls is wise.

There's no greater joy than saying, "That person, and that person, and that person—the Lord used me to win them to

Jesus." We've already talked about making a list of people you want to see saved. If you've been radically renewed, watch God begin to use you to win some of them to Jesus. It's a fantastic joy.

Your graduation is exciting. Your wedding is thrilling. The birth of your first child is exhilarating. But the most thrilling thing you and I can ever do is win someone to Jesus. Even the best the world has to offer is nothing compared to finding Jesus Christ and leading others to him.

I think of Fiona Hendley-Jones, an actress who shot to fame as one of the three robbers in a British television hit series known as "Widows." She later starred with Paul Jones in "The Beggar's Opera" and "Guys and Dolls."

Pop superstar Cliff Richard, a committed Christian, invited both Fiona and Paul to one of our evangelistic campaigns in London several years ago. They trusted Jesus and shortly thereafter were married. They joined a strong church and since have repeatedly commented in public appearances and media interviews about their new life in Christ.

"A lot of people turn to the church when they have torments in their life, but I was deliriously happy," Fiona explained while witnessing to one reporter. She told him how her life had "completely changed [when] I became a born-again Christian."

Fiona's testimony has helped lead many people to Jesus.

God wants to use each of us, famous or not, to tell others about the Good News. Your testimony may not be dramatic. Mine isn't. That doesn't matter. As Jesus told his disciples, let's simply rejoice that our names are written in the book of life as we tell others how they, too, can receive eternal life.

The Dutch evangelist Corrie ten Boom had a God-given desire to win others to Jesus. One of her poems is a favorite of mine. It says:

When I enter that beautiful city
And the saints all around me appear,
I hope that someone will tell me:
"It was you who invited me here."

Can you imagine? To get to heaven and meet someone who comes up and gives you a big hug and says, "Hey, I'm here because you invited me."

Nothing else could compare with that thrill!

Getting Started

You may be thinking, "Luis, how do I begin?" Why not begin with your interests and associations? If you're interested in football, befriend the people at your local school who play football. If you're in a carpool, pray for the others crammed in that car each morning. If you go to a health club, ask the Lord,

"Which of these people could I bring into the kingdom?"

If you enjoy fishing, invite a neighbor to go with you and pray for an opportunity to talk about the gospel. If you belong to a business or community group, pray to be used to win someone in that group to Jesus. If you host an exchange student from another country, you may have an excellent opportunity to witness for Jesus right in your own home.

If you work at an office or factory, you may know a dozen people or more who need Jesus in their life. The same is true if you're going to school. Pray for those you know by name. Don't rush to witness to the next person you meet. Begin to pray and the Holy Spirit will prompt you and give you an opportunity to share the love of Jesus with specific individuals.

Maybe a family is going through the heartache of divorce. When they mention it to you, invite them to pray with you. They may not be ready to follow Jesus on the spot. But by praying with them, they'll know you love them. Then watch for an opportunity to share the truth with them and point them toward Jesus.

If you're prayerfully alert, you may discover a large number of people around you who need Jesus. You may find incredible opportunities to witness.

I think of Martha in California who wrote to us, asking us to pray for her new neighbors, Dan and Annette. Before moving next door to Martha, this couple had never heard the gospel or read the Bible. Martha immediately befriended them, enlisted friends to pray for them, and then invited Annette over each week for an evangelistic Bible study.

Recently we received another letter from Martha. Her neighbor Annette has prayed to receive Jesus, she told us, "and now God is working in her husband's heart. Dan has attended worship services for the past three weeks and is desiring to know Jesus as his personal Savior as well." Praise God! You can know the same joy, too.

How Can We Remain Complacent?

If God is in our hearts, if he has blessed our life, if heaven is our home, how can we remain complacent about the destiny of our lost neighbors, relatives, and friends?

How can we care nothing about their present state? To think that the lost are happy "just as they are" is naive. They're lonely, hurting, desperate for love, and dying for a reason to live.

A young man in Toronto named Steve trusted Jesus several years ago. When we were back in that city a year later, one of my team members interviewed Steve about his conversion. "I remember that Friday night very well—January 15," he said. "Back then I was suicidal and bitter at life, at my family. I couldn't care about anything. When Luis said come on up, I jumped at the chance. Ever since then, I've been witnessing at my school—it's been a joy in my life. And a lot of people have become Christians. What happens is, you tell someone about Jesus and he becomes a Christian and tells someone else. Miracles happen!"

That same night, three more of Steve's friends trusted the Lord at a Youth for Christ rally where I spoke. It was exciting to hear his story and see how God has blessed him with so much fruit.

Yet today, in an effort to be sophisticated and contemporary, many Christians have stopped trying to persuade others to follow Jesus. There's an underlying feeling in our society that nice people don't go around persuading other people to do things. We don't want to offend people, appear strange, or lose our status. So we do nothing.

I, too, have been guilty of this. When we lived in Mexico City, my next-door neighbor was a young television personality. We would chat from time to time, and he even mentioned he listened to our radio program occasionally. But I didn't share the gospel with him. I was sure he was completely immune to the problems of life.

Eventually, though, my neighbor's situation changed. The joy seemed to have left his face. He and his wife started driving separate cars to work. I could tell their marriage was on the rocks, and I felt the need to talk with him, but I didn't want to meddle in his life. I went about my business and headed off for an evangelistic crusade in Peru. After all, that was the polite thing to do.

When I returned home, I learned my neighbor had killed himself. I was heartbroken. I knew I should have gone to him and persuaded him to repent and follow Jesus. But because of false courtesy—because I followed a social norm—I didn't do it.

It's very convenient to make excuses for not persuading others to follow Jesus. We may say we don't want to be overbearing or offensive. We may think we can't possibly witness to someone because he or she will become angry. But often the opposite is true.

I think of my daughter-in-law's experience as a college student. Michelle met a young woman who lived in the same apartment complex, and felt compelled to invite her to an evangelistic rally where I was speaking. And her neighbor agreed, just like that. Michelle didn't have to twist her arm or beg her or sell her on the idea. She just came, sat down, and listened to the gospel.

When I closed my message and gave the invitation, using Revelation 3:20, Michelle's new friend stood and almost ran forward to commit her life to Jesus. Later she said, "For years I've felt somebody knocking at the door of my heart, but I never knew who it was." Although she's a typical American, she had never heard the gospel until that night. And as soon as she heard it, she embraced it wholeheartedly.

Jesus longs to draw men and women to himself. So what holds us back from speaking to others in his name?

People Often Welcome the Gospel Message

Over the years I have learned that some of the people I thought would be most closed to the gospel often are the most receptive. Although they may outwardly fear it, in their hearts they welcome the message of the gospel.

I saw this while in the Soviet Union a few months before the dramatic collapse of communism in Eastern Europe. Christians in the Soviet Union, like other communist regions, had been persecuted for decades. Then, restrictions on evangelism were lifted. The situation I found there was incredible. I've traveled all over the world, but I've rarely seen a place as hungry and desperate to hear the gospel. Yet it took a while for many Soviet Christians to realize "the fields are white and ready to harvest."

Just before my evangelistic team's Soviet campaign was over, a Baptist pastor brought an acquaintance to one of our meetings in Moscow. The friend, a leading scientist and head of an academic department at the university, listened as I preached the gospel. Then, to the pastor's surprise, this scientist prayed out loud to receive Jesus as his Savior. And then, with tears, he came forward to confess Jesus as Lord publicly.

The Russian pastor was astonished at his friend's response to the gospel. He was equally surprised by the phone call he received at 7:15 the next morning. "I would like to express my gratitude to you," the scientist said. "You invited me to meet the Lord Jesus Christ. I didn't sleep the whole night. I just prayed. I asked God whether he would accept me, whether he would pardon me."

"Well, do you think God pardoned you?" the pastor asked.

His friend replied, "Yes, I'm absolutely sure that God accepts me as his prodigal son."

Later the pastor told me, "I never thought a scientist would accept the Lord Jesus as Savior. But now I've seen it with my own eyes. What a great experience!"

Why Do We Hold Back?

Having a part in leading a friend or acquaintance to faith in Jesus is exciting. Actually praying with someone who wants to make that decision, however, is even more thrilling. Yet I've seen Christians panic when talking with someone who's at the point of decision, ready to trust Jesus Christ.

A Christian woman was witnessing to a Hungarian

businesswoman sitting in front of me on a flight from Budapest to London. At the same time, our evangelistic association's European director and I were discussing the evangelistic rally we had in Budapest the day before with Cliff Richard.

While we were talking, the Christian woman stood up, turned around and said, "Excuse me. Are you talking about the rally yesterday with Cliff Richard and Luis Palau?" I said yes. "Do you know where brother Palau is?" she asked. With a smile, I told her that was me. Then she said, "I've been talking to this Hungarian lady, and I think she's ready to be converted. But I don't know how to do it."

I told her, "I've been listening to what you've been saying and you've done a terrific job." But she feared doing something wrong when it came time to pray with someone who was ready to follow Jesus. So I agreed to talk with the Hungarian businesswoman for a minute.

"Did you understand what this lady said to you?" I asked.

"Yes," said the Hungarian woman.

"Are you ready to follow Jesus with your whole heart?"

"Yes."

At that, I asked the Christian woman to lead her in a prayer of decision. I wanted to do it myself. It would have been great.

But instead, I sat back and watched as the Christian woman in front of me at first hesitated, then put her arm around this Hungarian woman, and for the first time led someone to Jesus.

I challenge you to pray: "Dear God, I want that experience. I want to know what it is to win someone to Jesus Christ."

Oh, to have a passion for the lost! Why should we be ashamed of the gospel? "It is the power of God for the salvation of everyone who believes" (Romans 1:16). It changes lives here and now, and for eternity. Whatever our place in the Body of Christ, let's work together to actively and prayerfully invite others into God's kingdom.

The Lord never intended the Christian life and witnessing to be a solo act. How can you and I prayerfully promote radical renewal and a passion for the lost within our churches, throughout our cities, and eventually across this country? How can we live out our faith in a way that changes our lives, and those around us? How can we find our way out of the normal, everyday struggles and proclaim His truth to a world in need?

That's the challenge ahead.

THE CHALLENGE AHEAD

8

God desires to radically renew you and me and lead us out of the desert. He wants to overcome our past. He wants to set us on a new path. And he's already begun the process.

You and I are on a pilgrimage. Our hearts are set toward renewal. And with that comes an increasingly intense passion for the things of God....

A passion for lost souls.

A passion for his word.

A passion for his creation.

And a passion for his followers.

We can't forget that God's plan is much bigger than his plan for you and me alone. In some ways, it's even bigger than his burden for the world. Yes, he earnestly desires to draw men and women and young people to himself. He is in the process of redeeming creation. But his Church stands directly at the center of his eternal plan.

So what's so special about the Church? From God's perspective...a lot.

We may look around at the tiny representative portion of the Church near us and get all worked up about the warts, wrinkles, and blemishes that haven't been taken care of yet.

But God sees the whole Church, throughout the world, down through the ages and into eternity. He views us not only as his special creation and masterpiece, but also as his family. God's ultimate goal is to perfect the Church and bring us all together (along with all the Old Testament saints) to spend eternity with him.

The highlight of eternity won't be the streets of gold. Instead, it's the fact that God wants to dwell with us forever (Revelation 20:3). He's not just satisfied to indwell us and fill us right now in this fallen world. He wants us to live "face to face" with him (1 Corinthians 13:12). "We shall be like him" in that day, "for we shall see him as he is" (1 John 3:2).

Granted, we in the Church aren't all we should be, or all we one day will be when we're with the Lord in glory. We have our struggles. We have our dirty little sins. We have our frustrations and pains. But that doesn't take away from the fact that he is doing a good work within us.

His goal is to renew both individuals and local churches as part of his overall plan here on earth—to make all things new.

If we really want to see renewal in our churches, and if we want to see God radically transform his followers across this country, we first must accept his work in our own lives. Otherwise, how can we promote what we ourselves haven't experienced? How can we present what we don't know and have?

Although I've talked a lot about "you and me," this book is meant for the whole Body of Christ. Writing these chapters has been good for me. I've had to pray, "Lord, am I living up to this message? I've enjoyed a Christ-centered life. I've seen great touches of renewal bless your Church in various places. But am I living at that same level today? Am I growing in my walk with you?"

I trust this book also has been used of God to make a tremendous impact in your own life. But don't be content to keep the principles of radical renewal to yourself. An independent, private, secretive Christianity can work, I suppose, but its progress is slow and discouragement is continual. The desert can be very dry. We are called to live out these biblical principles in our spheres of life.

God Always Starts with a Few

Wherever I've seen astounding moves of God, I can always trace it back to a small group of Christians who were broken over their sin, confessed it, were cleansed, and began a fresh walk with the indwelling Christ.

It has to start somewhere. Why not ask God to let it start with you?

I think of a small group I met with in England. They dreamed of seeing the churches of Britain renewed. Church leaders said

Great Britain hadn't experienced revival since a Billy Graham crusade in 1954. It was a genuine touch of God, but almost 26 years had passed. Now there was a foreboding deadness in many churches.

So a group of young men and women, many of them in their twenties, gathered to seek God's will. They scheduled a gathering on January 4, 1980, at the Royal Albert Hall in London. Their plan was to announce a decade of evangelism. "But before we can have evangelism," they told me, "we must have a touch of God."

The Royal Albert Hall was jammed with people that night, an impressive feat because London has few big churches. Many congregations number only 25, 30, or 40 people, many of them elderly.

I had just 30 minutes to speak that night. My theme was "Our God Reigns." Because I had to run through my message quickly to squeeze it into half an hour, it seemed unemotional. But to see the response! Many in the audience came forward to publicly dedicate their lives to Jesus. Some ministers, in tears, were among the first to the altar.

God began his work of renewal in many lives that night, and we saw the same response in nine other British cities. As a result, within four years the Lord allowed us to return to London for 14 weeks of evangelism, and Billy Graham came back for six campaigns in other cities. Previously, Dr. Graham had told how he was personally discouraged about future evangelistic work in Great Britain. Yet we saw tens of thousands of people give their lives to Jesus. And it all started with a touch of God among a few of his people.

Have you ever dreamed about what God wants to do—starting with you—in your church, in your city, in your world? I'm sure you've thought about the pain in the world. I'm sure you've dreamt about individuals half a world away, or half a block away, and quietly asked the Lord what he might be calling you to.

God wants to use you!

The biblical principles presented in this book are deep, yet simple. They're deep enough to challenge us for a lifetime, yet simple enough for most people to understand and apply immediately. And they work whether we're applying them here in this country or overseas.

Breakthrough

I've become even more convinced now than ever that God wants to renew his Church here in this country and around the world. I've seen it across Latin America and in parts of Europe and Asia. And I'm beginning to see it in North America.

Several years ago I met a Lutheran minister whose church saw someone come to the Lord almost every week. This pastor would be the first to admit that during his first eleven years of full-time ministry, he led only one person to Jesus—and he has doubts about that one.

God renewed this pastor while we were preparing for an evangelistic crusade in his city. He heard me present the principles outlined in this book and then completed our evangelistic association's training courses in friendship evangelism, counseling, and follow-up. He served as both a counselor and a pastoral advisor at the stadium meetings, helping many people clarify their public commitment to the Lord.

During the campaign, the pastor realized he had been preaching evangelism, but not practicing it. About a week later, that changed. During a premarital counseling session, he asked a young couple if they had eternal life. They said no. Instead of just talking to them about their need to follow Jesus, he invited them to make that decision right there in his office. Within six months, he had led more than 20 other people to Jesus.

What began as renewal in one pastor's life has produced a fabulous breakthrough in his church. And God has given him opportunities to help other churches experience spiritual and numerical growth, too.

"I don't think my feet have hit the ground yet," he remarked. "This is the beginning of a real revival for our congregation." That's the fruit of a renewed life overflowing with a passion for the things of God.

Imagine what God could do in your church, and my church, for his glory in coming weeks and months. Imagine what he could do in our lives—our families, our neighborhoods, our communities. We'll never know if we ignore the principles of spiritual renewal or keep them to ourselves.

If God renews you, you'll grow to love your church and pray for her. And you'll pray for the church around the world. You won't have a sectarian bone in your body.

Or if you do, you'll crucify it. Because if we're renewed, we're diligent to do whatever God commands. And one of the primary commands repeated eight times for us in the New Testament is to "love one another." That applies to all Christians, across the board, whether or not we agree on every point of doctrine and practice.

When I was younger, I used to preach certain minor points of doctrine with conviction. Now I'm embarrassed because after much further prayer and study I've changed my mind about a few of those details. What I'd learned earlier sounded good, but wasn't based squarely on a balanced view of God and his word. So I've grown. That's good. Let's leave room for others to grow, too.

Let's strive for the unity of the Body of Christ. Let's love our brothers and sisters in Christ, pray for them, and respect them as scripture commands. We won't see eye to eye on everything. But we can have unity because we were bought by the blood of the Savior, we're filled with his spirit, and we're preaching his scripture. That's our common ground, our basis for unity with all who are called by his name.

And as we reach out, as we serve others, as we preach his truth—God will deal with our own struggles, our own sin, and draw us close to him. He will renew us and set us on a radical new path. And your life will never be the same.

My prayer is that God will use this book to bless the whole Church, here in this country and around the world. May he renew us all and give us boldness as ambassadors of his son, Jesus Christ.

Now, let's make the most of the journey.

Psalm 57:8-11

"Awake, my soul! Awake, harp and lyre! I will awaken the dawn. I will praise you, Lord, among the nations; I will sing of you among the peoples. For great is your love, reaching to the heavens; your faithfulness reaches to the skies. Be exalted, O God, above the heavens; let your glory be over all the earth."

Luis Palau

For more than 50 years, Luis Palau has been a powerful spokesperson for the relevance, reality, and significance of spirituality for individuals around the world. His work has taken him to more than 75 nations and his campaigns have allowed him to present a clear case for Christianity to more than 1 billion people through television, radio, print, and live events.

Luis is known as one of the world's leading advocates for Christianity—standing strong for issues of faith and the importance of a vibrant, healthy spiritual life according to the teachings of the Bible. He is well regarded by leaders around the globe, including past presidents, church clergy, scientists, and business professionals.

Luis is the author of more than 40 books, host of three international daily radio programs, and head of the Luis Palau Association based in Portland, Oregon. He has dedicated his entire life and career to presenting the claims of Jesus Christ with as many people as possible.

For more information about Luis Palau and his ministry, visit www.palau.org.

Recommended Reading

To further enrich your spiritual life, look for the following books in your local bookstore or online.

Authentic Christianity by Ray C. Stedman (Multnomah Books)

Changed into His Likeness by Watchman Nee (Christian Literature Crusade)

Continuous Revival by Norman Grubb (Christian Literature Crusade)

Principles of Spiritual Growth by Miles Stanford (Back to the Bible)

Saving Life of Christ by W. Ian Thomas (Zondervan)

I love to browse for choice books in the used book section of bookstores, online, or in the libraries of veteran preachers and churches. Here are three out-of-print titles worth looking for:

The Passion for Souls by Oswald J. Smith

The Revival We Need by Oswald J. Smith

Rivers of Living Water by Ruth Paxson

Stay Connected

Luis Palau would love to hear from you. Please send your comments about this book or general thoughts on his ministry to:

Luis Palau
PO Box 50
Portland, Oregon 97207

You may also connect with him via:

Web: www.palau.org

Email: info@palau.org

Phone: 1.888.877.5847

Facebook: www.facebook.com/LuisPalauLive

Twitter: @LuisPalauLive

Partner in Ministry

Please consider making a significant and meaningful personal contribution to the work of evangelism by joining Luis Palau as a monthly financial partner through the *Champions for Change* partner program.

By joining Luis and his team through this powerful partner program, you will:

- Find encouragement, support, and tools you need to radically transform your own life and ministry

- Receive regular communication from Luis, inspiring words of encouragement, and online access to inspiring ministry resources

- Have the confidence of knowing you are sharing the hope of Jesus on a daily basis, strategically supporting sustainable, citywide evangelistic campaigns that impact communities, save lives, and further the kingdom of God

Find out more about the *Champions for Change* partner program and how you can play an active role in the work of evangelism at www.palau.org/champions.

NOTES

NOTES

NOTES